ARCTIC ANIMALS

Text by Jonquil Graves & Ed Hall.   Illustrations by Germaine Arnaktauyok

Northwest Territories Renewable Resources
The Honourable Nellie Cournoyea, Minister.
J.W. Bourque, Deputy Minister.

ISBN 0-7708-7139-9 $7.50

Illustrations: Germaine Arnaktauyok
Design: John Williamson

Order from:
   Department of Information
   Publications and Production Division
   Government of the Northwest Territories
   P.O. Box 1320
   Yellowknife, N.W.T. X1A 2L9

CONTENTS

FOREWORD

This publication deals with animals found above the treeline in the Northwest Territories. It provides line drawings, brief written accounts, and names in English, Inuktitut, and Latin, of a representative selection of mammals, birds, and fish. More complete listings of species are found in tables at the end of each of the three sections.

The scientific names for mammals follow Banfield's *Mammals of Canada* (1974); for birds, the 6th edition of the A.O.U. *Checklist of North American Birds* (1983); for freshwater fishes, Scott and Crossman's *Freshwater Fishes of Canada* (1973); and for marine fishes, Leim and Scott's *Fishes of the Atlantic Coast of Canada* (1966).

The Inuktitut words are a mixture of those used in the Keewatin and the Baffin. These words are given in syllabics and Roman orthography, and conform with the Inuit Cultural Institute's standard spellings. However, due to the varied usage throughout the Northwest Territories, there are bound to be differences of opinion about some of the words here. Interested individuals are invited to add to the record any Inuktitut names not included (or to correct any errors), by writing to:

Supervisor, Conservation Education
Dept. of Renewable Resources
Government of the Northwest Territories
Yellowknife, N.W.T. X1A 2P9

Canada's heritage of arctic wildlife is a treasure beyond reckoning. It is hoped this brief volume will bring that treasure to a wider audience, and add to everyone's enjoyment of it.

ACKNOWLEDGEMENTS

This publication is based upon Joanne Coutu's *Animals of the Eastern Arctic: A Checklist in English and Inuktitut,* which was sponsored by several departments of the Government of the Northwest Territories (including Education, Information, and Renewable Resources). Since its appearance in Rankin Inlet in 1981, the original volume has been much in demand; however, since only a limited number of copies was printed, much of that demand went unsatisfied.

The present volume has been renamed *Arctic Animals.* All the sketches have been redone and brief written accounts added. But since it owes so much to Joanne Coutu's work, it is only fitting we reprint here her original acknowledgements:

> *I am particularly grateful to Dr. Cormack Gates for his guidance, advice and suggestions throughout the entire project. My special thanks are also extended to the people of the Keewatin and Arctic Bay for their infinite patience in providing me with the correct Inuktitut terms for each animal in this book. Here are but a few names: my father- and mother-in-law, Marc Tungilik and his wife Angugatsiak, Lionel Angotingoar and his wife Ullattiaq from Repulse Bay, Leo Ussak and his wife Arnaqjuaq from Rankin Inlet, Nasuk Alooloo from Arctic Bay. I also thank Leonie Kappi and Ray Sateanna for typing and transcribing the Roman orthography into syllabics. Last but not least, I wish to thank my husband, Marius Tungilik, who facilitated my communication with the people.*

Arctic Animals too is the result of hard work by many people behind the scenes. Paul Wilson (formerly of the Dept. of Information) had the vision to see the publication in its present form and was instrumental in getting the project started. Betty Harnum of the Language Bureau provided able and diligent assistance in editing the Inuktitut portion. Many people helped in reviewing the English text, including (from the Dept. of Renewable Resources) Bob Bromley, Cormack Gates, Bruce Stephenson, Cathy Stephenson, and expecially Bob Ferguson, whose patience and helpful comments went beyond the call of duty; while other staff members, including Mike Ferguson and Seemega Aqpik, assisted in collecting Inuktitut names in the Baffin region. Brian Wong of the Dept. of Fisheries and Oceans in Yellowknife rendered cheerful assistance in tracking down helpful information. D.F.O. personnel in Winnipeg reviewed the sections on fish and marine mammals, and their comments were invaluable in improving the quality of the book — though any errors in these sections remain our own responsibility. Finally, the expert typing of Ellen Christensen and Anna Milligan made the task of manuscript preparation immeasurably easier.

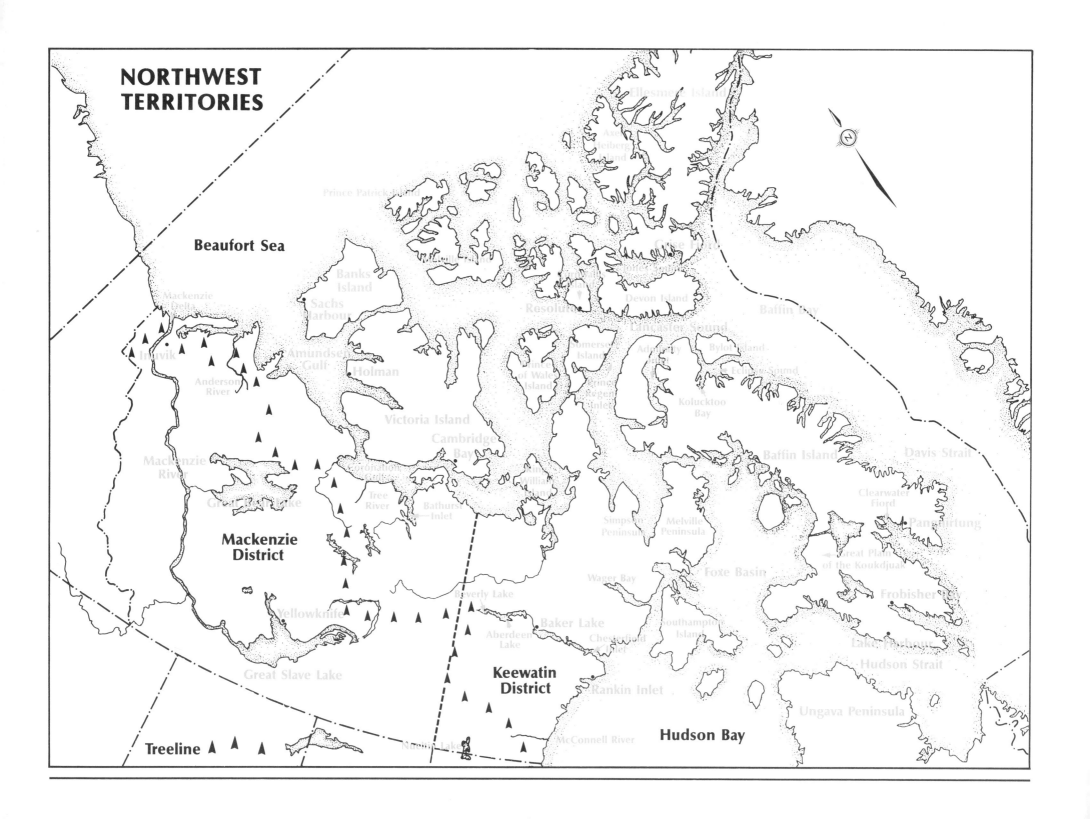

NORTHWEST TERRITORIES

Beaufort Sea

Prince Patrick Island

Ellesmere Island

Axel
Heiberg
Island

Banks
Island

Sachs
Harbour

Devon Island

Baffin Bay

Resolute

Lancaster Sound

Amundsen
Gulf

Holman

Somerset
Island

Admiralty
Inlet

Bylot Island

Echo Sound

Mackenzie
Delta

Inuvik

Anderson
River

Prince
of Wales
Island

Prince
Regent
Inlet

Kolucktoo
Bay

Victoria Island

Cambridge
Bay

Baffin Island

Davis Strait

Mackenzie
River

Coronation
Gulf

King
William
Island

Clearwater
Fiord

Great Bear Lake

Tree
River

Bathurst
Inlet

Simpson
Peninsula

Melville
Peninsula

Pangnirtung

**Mackenzie
District**

Great Plain
of the Koukdjuak

Yellowknife

Beverly Lake

Wager Bay

Foxe Basin

Frobisher Bay

Baker Lake

Aberdeen
Lake

Chesterfield
Inlet

Southampton
Island

Lake Harbour

Great Slave Lake

**Keewatin
District**

Rankin Inlet

Hudson Strait

Nueltin Lake

McConnell River

Ungava Peninsula

Hudson Bay

Treeline ▲ ▲ ▲

MAMMALS

MAMMALS

Mammals have adapted to an amazing variety of habitats and lifestyles, establishing themselves on land, air and sea. It is this adaptability which is responsible for their success as a life form. Nor should it be surprising that, found among this highly versatile group, are the most intelligent of all animals.

Despite their differences, all mammals share the same basic characteristics: they breathe air, they have warm blood, they bear their young live, and they nurture their newborn offspring with mother's milk. All of these features represent evolutionary advances over earlier life forms.

Out of several thousand species of mammals in the world, there are about 200 in Canada. There are even fewer in the Northwest Territories, since the diversity of species decreases northward due to the harshness of the climate. Above the treeline there are only 20 mammalian species which regularly inhabit the land mass.

This means that arctic food chains are less diversified and therefore more fragile, and that disrupting influences can have serious and widespread consequences. Perhaps this is why some arctic species, such as lemmings, hares and foxes, experience dramatic population fluctuations. It is also the reason why man must exercise considerable caution in his desire to develop the north. To our credit (there are always a few exceptions and always room for improvement), the record of our concern in arctic Canada is heartening. Each year several million dollars are spent by various agencies for the benefit of wildlife in the Northwest Territories.

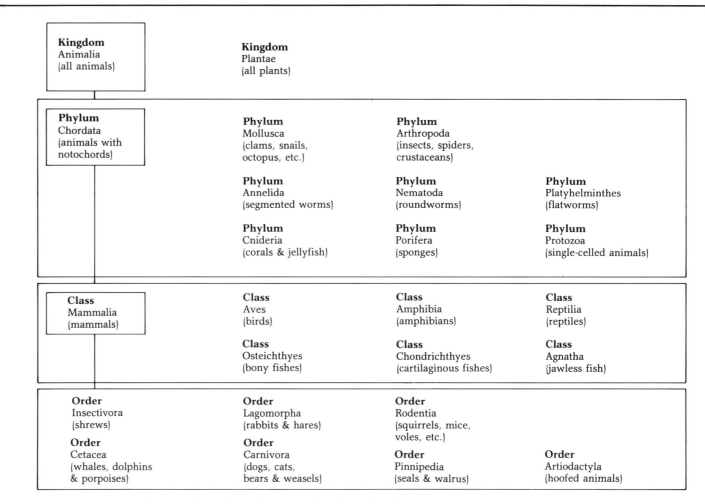

Simplified diagram showing mammalian orders with representatives found above the treeline in the Northwest Territories, and their relationship to other organisms.

Just as some plant and animal species are used as indicators by scientists in monitoring the accumulation of harmful substances in an ecosystem, so some observers see the success or failure of our wildlife programs as an indication of man's own development, and ultimately the future of the world.

MUSKOX

To see a muskox is to look back into prehistoric times, for these animals are creatures of the last ice age. Prior to the arrival of Europeans in North America, muskoxen roamed the tundra in large numbers, but in the last century they were greatly reduced by the insatiable demands of explorers, fur traders and whalers for meat and hides. Finally, in 1917, hunting and trading in hides was prohibited. In 1927 the Thelon Game Sanctuary was created to preserve what was thought to be one of the few remaining populations on the mainland. Since then the species has rebounded from a low of about 10,000 animals to about 45,000 in 1982.

Muskoxen in the Northwest Territories now form a majority of the world population. They are found on most arctic islands, except Baffin Island, and on the mainland they occur along the arctic coast, in some areas as far south as the treeline. They are generally restricted to locations where annual snow depths do not exceed 50 cm. In summer they prefer river valleys, lakeshores and damp meadows where they feed on willows, sedges and grasses. In winter they move to hilltops, plateaus and gravel eskers where berries, birch, willows and labrador tea are blown clear of snow.

Muskoxen are bulky animals with a prominent shoulder hump. An average bull weighs about 350 kg and a cow about 300 kg. Both sexes bear horns. The coat is composed of a dense undergarment of wool overlain by long guard hairs which hang down to the knees like a skirt. On the back is a pale spot or saddle. In April or early May, the muskoxen become tatty or ill-kempt as their winter coats begin to moult. The wool is shed in mats and streamers, with new growth beginning in summer.

Muskoxen are gregarious animals, grouping together in mixed herds whose size depends on season, range and breeding condition. Winter herds tend to be larger than summer ones, although in the case of harassment by helicopters and vehicles, herds may temporarily fragment. When threatened by wolves, muskoxen form a characteristic ring or semi-circle with bulls and cows facing outwards, and calves and yearlings in the centre or wedged safely between the adults.

Herds are generally led by a dominant bull, or a cow if bulls are absent. The dominant bull shows leadership in times of stress and is also responsible for mating with most of the cows in the herd. Breeding occurs in August and September with much fighting and charging among bulls.

Calves are born in April or May and are extremely precocious, standing and nursing within an hour of birth. They remain with their mothers until after their first winter. Young female muskoxen do not breed until they are 3 years old and bulls are not mature until the age of 5. Only single calves are born.

The expanding muskox population in the Northwest Territories has been the source of two transplants. In 1967, 15 animals were moved from Ellesmere Island to Quebec for a domestication project. In 1974, 10 muskoxen were captured on Banks Island and flown to Russia. In those areas of the Northwest Territories where muskox populations can support hunting, quotas have been allotted.

MUSKOX	ᐅᒥᖕᒪᒃ	Umingmak	*Ovibos moschatus*
Calf	ᐅᒥᖕᒫᒃ	Umingmaak	
Yearling (male or female)	ᑑᓕᒐᖅ	Tuuligaq	
2-year-old female	ᑰᕋᕝᕕᐊᕋᖅ	Kuuravviaraq	
Female with calf	ᐅᒥᖕᒫᓕᒃ	Umingmaalik	
Female without a calf, or dry cow	ᐅᒥᖕᒪᐃᑦᑐᖅ	Umingmaittuq	
Young bull	ᓯᒡᓕᖅᑕᐅᑎᓕᒃ	Sigliqtautilik	
Mature bull	ᐊᖑᔾᔪᐊᖅ	Angujjuaq	

CARIBOU

Two subspecies of caribou are found above the treeline: barren-ground caribou (*R.t. groenlandicus*) and Peary caribou *(R.t. pearyii)*.

Barren-ground caribou is the subspecies which forms great herds and undertakes spectacular migrations. At least four major herds have been identified on the mainland: Bluenose, Bathurst, Beverly and Kaminuriak. Generally these herds winter below the treeline and migrate onto the barrens for spring and summer. The northward migration is led by cows returning to traditional calving areas where most give birth to a single calf in June. The calves are able to stand and walk within an hour of birth, and soon after are following their mothers across the tundra. Throughout the summer the caribou are on the move and feeding constantly to build up strength for the coming winter. By October, when the rut occurs, they are usually near the treeline. Bulls brandish their antlers and spar with each other to earn the right to breed.

From November to March or April the herds move slowly through their wintering range in the boreal forest. Then, with pregnant cows leading the way north, the cycle is repeated. Animals which were calves the previous spring will soon be abandoned by their mothers, who must focus their attention on the arrival of new calves. Males achieve adult weights of 105-145 kg by 5 years of age, and females 80-90 kg by 3 years. These weights fluctuate throughout the course of the year. Most females are breeding by the age of 3½ years, though some breed earlier.

Not all barren-ground caribou winter in the boreal forest; some remain on the tundra. In addition, the subspecies is found on Baffin Island, where there are no trees. Little is known about the caribou occupying the north half of the island. In the south half there is a large migratory herd which mimics the north-south movements of its counterparts on the mainland, but there are also some areas where caribou are found year-round.

Peary caribou are smaller than barren-ground caribou and lighter in colour. They are found only on the arctic islands, on and between which they seasonally migrate. They are considered "threatened" due to declines inflicted by severe winter conditions.

Caribou numbers have always been an area of interest and contention. Early explorers guessed at millions and created a false impression of plenty. At mid-century when the first scientific techniques of estimating numbers were applied, it was discovered that the herds had declined drastically. Since then the trend has been reversed, with most herds of barren-ground caribou either stable or increasing.

Caribou traditionally provided food and many other necessities to the people of the north. Caribou hides were necessary for bedding and clothing, while tools and utensils were fashioned from antler and bone. Caribou meant the difference between life and death for many Inuit and Dene, and even today some northerners rely significantly on caribou meat. Consequently, the ultimate goal of the government is to manage the herds at a level which permits both hunting and conservation.

Caribou management in the Northwest Territories involves surveying herds to determine numbers, collecting harvest data, protecting critical areas from disturbance, and regulating commercial and sport hunting. A recent innovation has been the formation of caribou management boards wherein native northerners can participate in the decision-making process.

CARIBOU	ᑐᒃᑐ	Tuktu	*Rangifer tarandus*
Calf	ᓄᕐᕋᖅ	Nurraq	
Calf, first winter	ᓄᕐᕋᕕᓂᖅ	Nurraviniq	
Yearling	ᑎᖅᐳᕐᖅ/ᑎᕆᑐᕐᖅ	Tiqituraq / Tirituraq	
2-year-old male	ᓄᒃᑐᒐᖅ	Nukatugaq	
3-year-old male	ᐊᖑᓴᓗᖅ	Angusalluq	
Young bull	ᐅᓱᐊᓕᒡᔪᐊᖅ	Usualigjuaq	
Mature bull	ᐸᖕᓂᖅ	Pangniq	
Female with calf	ᓄᕐᕋᓕᒃ	Nurralik	
Dry cow, immature female without calf	ᖅᓄᕐᕋᐃᑦᑐᖅ	Nurraittuq	

MOOSE

Although moose are generally found below the treeline, their range also extends onto the tundra. They have been observed as far east as Baker Lake, north to Bathurst Inlet, and at the arctic coast around Amundsen Gulf.

The moose is the largest member of the deer family. Bulls weigh about 500 kg but may reach as much as 850 kg. Cows are generally lighter, but both male and female adults stand about 2 m at the shoulder. Males have large antlers which start to develop in their first autumn. Huge racks weighing up to 32 kg do not form until the bull is 4 or 5 years old. The antlers are shed every year in early winter, and by late August or early September have again attained full size.

Moose are solitary animals. Mating season in the fall is the usual time that males and females are found together. There may be some socialization at other seasons too, in areas of concentrated food sources. Calves are born in the spring and remain with their mothers until the following spring. At that time yearlings may join up with a bull or another of the same age, but such unions are temporary and the adolescents soon establish home ranges of their own.

MOOSE   ⊃ᵇ⊃ᐸᵇ   Tuktuvak   *Alces alces*

Above the treeline two types of wolves are generally recognized: arctic wolves, which inhabit the arctic islands, and tundra wolves, which are found on the mainland. Tundra wolves reach weights of 40 kg for males and 32 kg for females, while arctic wolves are smaller. The two types also differ in colour. Arctic wolves generally have white silky coats, while tundra wolves vary from white to brown, grey or black.

A wolf's diet depends on the season and availability of food in the area. It could include hares, foxes, rodents, birds, fish, eggs, garbage, or even small quantities of vegetable matter. However, the usual fare of all wolves is big game. On the mainland tundra, wolves prey almost exclusively on caribou, which they follow from summer ranges in the barrens to the boreal forest in winter. In the high arctic, they hunt both caribou and muskox.

Wolves have no natural predators in the Northwest Territories, but because they prey on caribou and other big game, they have in the past been subjected to various control programs, including bounty payments (mainly in the 1920's and 1930's) and poisoning (mainly in the 1950's). Currently they

WOLF ◁L ?⁵ᵇ Amaruq *Canis lupus*

are hunted and trapped with few restrictions. Despite these pressures, wolves still occupy all of their traditional range in the Northwest Territories — a tribute to their resourcefulness.

The red fox occurs over all of mainland Northwest Territories. In 1918 or 1919, red foxes crossed Hudson Strait from Ungava to southern Baffin Island and by the late 1940's had spread over all of Baffin Island. In 1962 they crossed Lancaster Sound and reached Resolute Bay on Cornwallis Island and Grise Fiord on Ellesmere Island. They are also found on Southampton Island.

Red foxes belong to the same family as wolves and dogs (*Canidae*). An average male weighs about 5.5 kg and stands 355 mm at the shoulder. Vixens (female foxes) are slightly smaller. Although most red foxes are golden-red, there are a number of colour variations or phases. These are the silver fox (black with silver-tipped guard hairs), black fox (all black) and cross fox (brownish with a dark cross over the shoulders). Despite their names, all belong to the same species and a single litter may contain more than one colour phase.

Red foxes are thought to mate for life and occupy the same home range. In late winter the pair digs a new den, renovates a discarded one, or finds a suitable crevice or cave. Whelps are born in late spring and litter size is dependent on the availability of prey species, particularly lemmings. In a good lemming year, litters may have as many as 25 whelps, while in a poor year few young will be born, or only a few foxes will breed.

As the whelps are growing, both parents bring food, and in late summer teach them how to hunt for themselves. By autumn, the young foxes are independent and go their separate ways, travelling singly until February when the breeding season brings new mates together.

Arctic foxes are adventuresome travellers, covering great distances on hunting trips. Sometimes they are found on the sea ice where they drift with the floes, returning to shore far from their starting place. In this way, all the arctic islands have become populated with foxes. On the mainland their range extends throughout the barrens and somewhat below the treeline.

The foxes are active all year long, denning only during the whelping season or for brief periods in temporary dens during blizzards. In winter they hunt lemmings, arctic hares and ptarmigan, and feed on carrion left behind by wolves and polar bears. In summer foxes may fare exceptionally well on eggs stolen from nests on the ground or cliffs, and by hunting gulls, loons, ptarmigan, small birds and rodents. Near the coast they eat food such as sea urchins, crabs and molluscs, and are adept at catching fish.

Arctic fox populations are cyclic, and severe declines (called "crashes") often follow a year after the disappearance of lemmings. In years when food is plentiful, foxes breed earlier and may have large litters, but in poor food years only some foxes breed and litters of four or six are more common.

All foxes are susceptible to rabies, encephalitis and distemper. For this reason people should never feed foxes or otherwise encourage their close approach, however tame they may appear. Trappers should wear disposable rubber gloves when skinning foxes, and afterwards wash hands and knives in warm soapy water.

Trapping arctic foxes is an important activity for many people in the north, in particular for the Inuit living in coastal settlements on the mainland, where it represents a major source of income. Foxes are trapped during the winter when their coats are white or "blue" (actually blue-black to pearl grey). By early March the brown summer coat begins to appear, and looks ragged and mottled until the beginning of July. The arctic fox is the only member of the family *Canidae* whose coat changes colour seasonally.

RED FOX (left)	ᓈᓚᓂᐊᕐᔪᒃ	Tiriganiarjuk	*Vulpes vulpes*
	ᑲᔪᐊᓗᒃ	Kajualuk (qitirmiut)	
	ᑲᔪᖅ	Kajuq	
	ᑲᔪᖅᑐᖅ	Kajuqtuq	

| ARCTIC FOX (right, in winter coat) | ᓈᓚᓂᐊᖅ | Tiriganiaq | *Alopex lagopus* |

Polar bears are among the largest of all bears. Females grow until they are about 4 years old and weigh up to 300 kg. Males grow until about 8 years of age, attaining weights of 450-600 kg and lengths of 2.5-3.5 m from nose to tail. Some individuals have grown even larger.

Polar bears are the most carnivorous of all bears, but like their ursine relatives will eat nearly anything. Their preference, however, is for ringed and bearded seals. Occasionally walrus, beluga and narwhal are eaten, although these species are rarely killed by bears, but found as carrion along the shore.

Polar bears range throughout the arctic and subarctic from the permanent pack ice of the Arctic Ocean to southern James Bay. In summer they seek out areas of permanent ice, drift about on ice floes, or come ashore at traditional retreats. To avoid overheating they are less active during the summer. They prey on birds and rodents, consume vegetation, and scavenge the beaches. When the sea ice reforms, they venture out on it again to resume hunting seals. During the winter, unlike other species of bears, only pregnant females den up for extended periods.

Mating occurs in spring, but because of "delayed implantation" the embryo does not begin to develop until September. In November or December the female excavates a snow den, often on a south-facing hill near the coast. Some of the best known denning areas are on southern Banks Island, Simpson Peninsula, Southampton Island and eastern Baffin Island.

Cubs, usually twins, are born sometime between late November and January. In March or April they leave their dens and usually accompany their mothers for at least 2½ years. Such a long mother-cub relationship, and the fact that female bears are not sexually mature until at least 4 years of age, means that polar bears have one of the lowest birth rates of all arctic animals.

Earlier in this century when polar bear populations were thought to be declining, government took the first steps toward conservation by limiting the annual hunting season in 1935, and by restricting hunting to native people in 1949. Community quotas were instituted in 1967, and in 1976 an international agreement to conserve polar bears came into effect. The agreement binds all five countries where polar bears are found — Canada, Greenland, Norway, Russia and the United States.

Polar bear populations are now believed to be stable or increasing in most areas of Canada. In the Northwest Territories, where most of the world's polar bears are found, annual research is carried out to determine numbers and distribution. This information is used to adjust community quotas, which total about 600 bears per year.

When entering the polar bear's domain, one is well advised not to be deceived by the animal's customary shambling gait and ponderous movements. A creature of enormous strength, perseverance and ingenuity, it is also capable of frightening bursts of speed. In polar bear country one must always remain alert and not invite harm by carelessly storing food or garbage. Polar bears have, without provocation, attacked and killed human beings in the Northwest Territories — though they are far less in number than those bears who each year are lured into dangerous situations by irresponsible humans, and then slain.

POLAR BEAR	ᓇᓄᖅ	Nanuq	*Ursus maritimus*
Newborn in den	ᐊᑎᖅᑕᓛᖅ	Atiqtalaaq	
Cub, when able to accompany mother	ᐊᑎᖅᑕᖅ/ᓇᓄᐊᓛᖅ	Atiqtaq / Nanualaaq	
Female with cubs	ᐊᑎᖅᑕᓕᒃ	Atiqtalik	
Adult male	ᐊᖑᔾᔪᐊᖅ	Angujjuaq	

BARREN-GROUND GRIZZLY

The term barren-ground grizzly is used to refer to a distinct population of grizzly bears which, in the Northwest Territories, occurs over northern and eastern Mackenzie and central Keewatin.

The distinguishing features of the grizzly are a slightly dished face, a prominent hump and long ruff of hair on the shoulders, and extremely long claws. Colour ranges from creamy-yellow to almost pure black, with pale bears being the most common in the barrens.

Grizzlies have a reputation for ferocity earned for the most part from too many encounters with humans in southern national parks. In areas where they have not become habituated to man, they are often shy, either fleeing immediately or minding their own business. However, surprised or cornered bears have been known to injure and kill. Thus, the cardinal rule is to show great respect for these powerful animals, keep your eyes open in bear country and stay out of their way.

Grizzly bears are omnivorous. In spring, they graze on new grasses, sedges, and roots, and switch to berries in summer and fall. They also eat lemmings and ground squirrels which they excavate from burrows. With respect to large game animals, bears are opportunistic predators and will kill caribou, moose and muskoxen if the occasion arises. They also feed on any carcasses they find, remaining in the vicinity of the carrion until it is completely cleaned up.

Mating occurs from late spring to early summer and cubs are born when the female is in her winter den. The young remain with their mother for a second winter and then may den together by themselves in the third year. The female may or may not mate again that year. This rather long inter-litter period, together with the small litter size (the average is less than two cubs) and the late sexual maturity (6-7 years) means that grizzly bears are susceptible to over-hunting. As a result, only native people are permitted to hunt barren-ground grizzlies. Hunting is for subsistence only, except in a few instances where small community quotas have been allocated.

LYNX

The lynx is the only wild cat found in the Northwest Territories. A fully grown lynx is 80-90 cm long and weighs up to 18 kg. Males are larger than females. The fur of the lynx, much in demand by trappers, is long, thick, and soft. It is a greyish buffy colour slightly spotted with brown.

Although generally restricted to thick boreal forest, lynx may venture onto the tundra during lean years in search of arctic hares, lemmings, and ptarmigan. There is an extralimital sighting of one on Baffin Island.

Lynx are solitary animals occupying a home range of 15 to 20 sq. km. Within that range they are active all year round, except in the most extreme weather conditions when they wait out storms or low temperatures under a log or branch of a tree. They are nocturnal and spend the night prowling along hare runways or waiting in ambush for their favourite meal, the snowshoe hare.

Lynx subsist almost entirely on hares and may kill up to 200 each year. But such a limited diet has its

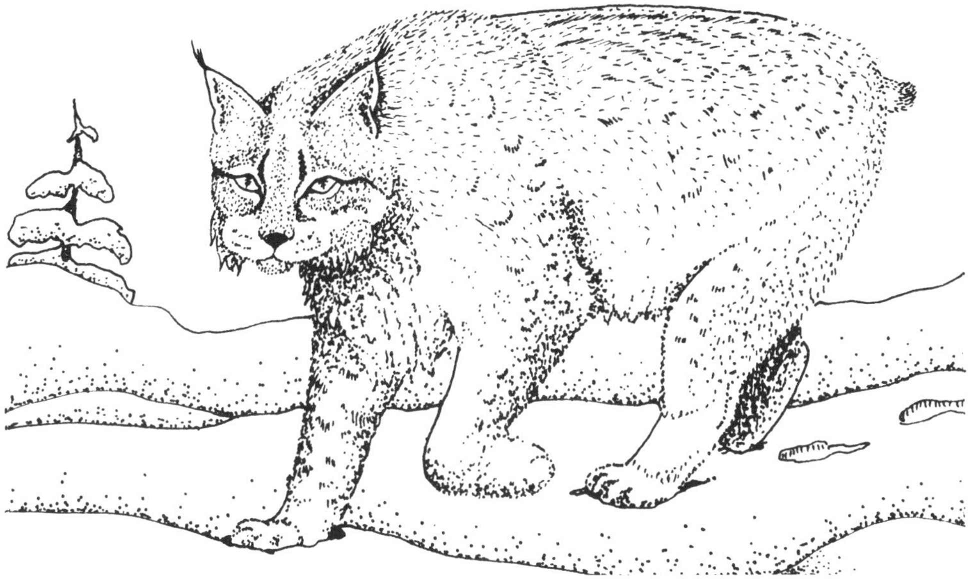

BARREN-GROUND GRIZZLY ᐊᒃᖤᖅ Akłaq *Ursus arctos*
ᐊᒃᖤ Akła

LYNX ᐱᖅᑐᖅᓯᕋᖅ Piqtuqsiraq *Lynx lynx*

pitfalls, for in years of hare crashes, which occur about 10 years apart, the lynx goes hungry and populations decline. Although adult lynx do not usually starve, litter sizes are smaller, many females do not conceive at all and if they do, the kittens die from lack of nourishment.

In normal years, conception usually occurs in March or April. Two to three kittens are born 9 weeks later in May or June. Kittens are brought up entirely by their mother, the male lynx having departed soon after mating. The family stays together throughout the winter and each member goes its separate way in spring.

ERMINE

Ermine are small carnivores whose size belies their ferocity. An average male weighs about 80 g and a female 55 g. Despite their diminutive bodies, ermines prove a match for small hares, ground squirrels, pikas and birds. Because it is almost without fear, a cornered ermine will attack anything, even a man or a dog. The ermine strikes with lightning speed, usually aiming to bite through the muscles of the neck just below the head. If the victim is large, the ermine may be thrown off its feet, but the strong jaws and sharp teeth enable it to hold fast.

Ermine take full advantage of any kill by either hiding with it in a den and feasting until all is gone, or by eating sparingly and storing the excess. Towards the beginning of winter it is usual for an ermine to stock a larder with small rodents such as mice and lemmings.

Ermine are equally at home in the boreal forest, the tundra, and the high arctic. They usually stay close to cover and can be observed running fluidly in and out of crevices, in boulder fields, or darting through the dead trees and foliage of the forest floor. They seem undaunted by all terrain and climb trees, swim streams, and cross frozen ponds with equanimity. They are active in summer and winter, and although primarily nocturnal in the south, are seen during all the long daylight hours of the arctic summer.

In response to lengthening or shortening daylight, ermine coats change colour with the seasons. The summer coat is brown and the winter coat is white except for a black tip at the end of the tail.

WOLVERINE

Wolverines may be found throughout the mainland Northwest Territories and on some arctic islands, including Banks, Victoria, Melville, and Little Cornwallis. They are not particularly abundant over any part of their range.

Wolverines are solitary animals and will not tolerate the presence of another of the same sex on their territory. Males and females associate briefly during the mating season which extends from April until September. Two to five cubs are born between mid-March and late April. It is thought that this rather small litter size, together with the fact that females do not mate until their second or third summer and may not breed every year, contributes to the relatively low number of wolverines.

The availability of food also determines abundance and distribution of wolverine populations. They are primarily scavengers and often follow caribou herds to clean up carcasses left by wolves and bears. Wolverines do occasionally kill large game; however, they are not particularly efficient hunters. In deep snow their large paws combined with a comparatively light body give them some advantage, but on bare ground, a healthy moose or caribou can easily outdistance the clumsy gallop of a wolverine. In addition to lemmings, ground squirrels, and fish, they also eat roots and berries, and where man is present, steal from his camps, caches, and traplines.

Wolverines are noted for their ferocity and have been known to defend their food against a bear or wolf. They have no hesitation about putting an inquisitive dog to flight and will attack a man if cornered.

Wolverine pelts are particularly valued for parka hoods because the long guard hairs prevent the fur from frosting up.

ERMINE (left, in winter coat)	ᏆᎾᐊᓈ	Tiriaq	*Mustela erminea*
WOLVERINE (right)	ᑫᐸᐱᐦ ᑫᐸᐱᒡᓴᒡ	Qavvik Qavvigaarjuk	*Gulo gulo*

ARCTIC HARE

There are no rabbits in the Northwest Territories, only hares. The treeline forms an approximate boundary between the range of the arctic hare and the snowshoe hare. The arctic hare is found throughout the tundra on the mainland and on all arctic islands. In the southern part of their range, the hares change colour seasonally, moulting to grey or brown in summer, while farther north they remain white all year round.

Arctic hares are found in rocky areas and on rough hillsides, usually in large groups which consist of small family units on the mainland to large herds of 100 or more in the high arctic.

In some places arctic hare may be migratory. Around the Nueltin Lake area in the Keewatin, they disappear during the summer and reappear from the north in November after freeze-up. Arctic hare populations are also cyclic and their abundance or scarcity affects their predators.

Hares feed on grasses, sedges, willows and other plants. In summer they browse along slowly, crouched on all four feet, while in winter they

ARCTIC HARE (upper left)	▷ᛒᑎᕐᖅ ▷ᛒᑎᐊᕐᔪᒃ	Ukaliq Ukaliarjuk	*Lepus arcticus*
MASKED SHREW (lower left)	▷ᒡᔪᖕᓇᖅ	Ugjungnaq	*Sorex cinereus*
ARCTIC GROUND SQUIRREL (lower right)	ᓯᒃᓯᒃ	Siksik	*Spermophilus parryii*

break through the snow crust with their forepaws, dig with the aid of their long curved claws and push the snow aside with their noses to reach the vegetation underneath. Hares do not hibernate in winter, but may take temporary refuge from blizzards in dens excavated in snowbanks and in the lee of boulders.

Baby hares, called leverets, are born in June in a simple nest on the ground. They are well-developed at birth and are fully grown by September. Some females, or does, may have more than one litter in a summer.

MASKED SHREW

The masked shrew is found throughout the mainland Northwest Territories. It is one of the most common and widely distributed mammals, but because of its small size and secretive lifestyle, it is rarely seen.

Masked shrews are about 10 cm in length and have a long nose, small eyes and ears, small clawed feet, and a long thin tail. The coat varies in colour from grey to dull brown; it moults in the spring and again in the fall.

Shrews are short-lived creatures: their lifespan is about 14-16 months. Active 24 hours a day, they lead a fast-paced existence which is centred on food-gathering. In the wild they eat their own weight in food in a single day, and in captivity may eat three times that much. Although their food consists chiefly of insects in all stages, they are ferocious hunters willing to attack anything they can chew and swallow.

Young shrews are born between spring and fall, and females may produce two or three litters in a season. The young are born in a nest concealed under a log, a stone, or a stump. In a few weeks young shrews are ready to leave the nest and mark out their own territories, although most do not breed until the following spring.

Shrews are loners except during mating time. They are staunch defenders of their nest and territories, screaming in shrill voices at intruders and chasing them off.

Shrews are useful to man in that they eat large numbers of insects, and they themselves are a food item for larger species such as weasels, hawks and owls.

ARCTIC GROUND SQUIRREL

The most common arctic ground squirrel in the Northwest Territories is the subspecies, *S.p. parryii*. It is a large (700-800 g), dark brown rodent found on the tundra from the Anderson River in northwestern Mackenzie to Melville Peninsula and Hudson Bay in the Keewatin.

The arctic ground squirrel has a dappled, greyish-brown back with tawny-coloured underparts. The head, cheeks, and shoulders are also tawny-coloured and the tail a mixture of black and brown. The soft fur is valued for making warm parka linings and mitts.

Arctic ground squirrels are generally found in areas where they can excavate extensive burrows. Places which are free from permafrost, such as eskers, sand banks, and boulder fields, all provide good habitat for ground squirrel colonies.

The arctic ground squirrel spends about 7 months of the year hibernating in an underground den which is part of a maze of tunnels up to 18 m long. Hibernation begins in September or October and continues through to April or May. Males usually emerge first, often when the ground is still covered in snow. For the first few weeks the squirrels stay close to their dens, feeding on stores of willow leaves and seeds cached the previous fall. When the snow melts and new growth forms, the squirrels begin to wander farther afield.

Breeding occurs in late May and young squirrels are born in mid to late June. They spend the summer feeding on flowers, berries, grasses, and any carrion they can find. They also become nuisances in camps, begging and scrounging for food.

Ground squirrels are an important source of food for wolves, arctic foxes, grizzly bears and ermine. Raptors, such as hawks and falcons, also prey on the young animals.

LEMMINGS

Lemmings look like large prosperous mice without tails. They have big heads, flat bodies, and weigh from 60 to 90 g. Their round appearance is further emphasized by their apparent lack of ears and feet, both of which are small and hidden by dense fur.

The pelage of both the brown and collared lemming is long, thick and silky. During the summer months, both lemmings are similar in buffy-grey to chestnut-brown coats, but in winter the collared lemming turns snow-white — the only rodent to do so.

Both species are found throughout the tundra on the mainland. The collared lemming occurs on all arctic islands, while the brown lemming is absent from the most northerly ones.

Lemmings prefer moist areas where they can excavate small burrows and runways through the vegetation. In summer, collared lemmings are usually found in drier, rockier places than brown lemmings, but both species winter in low marshy country where sedges and cottongrass catch the snow and provide a good layer of insulation over the nests and tunnels.

Both types are active all winter beneath the snow and collared lemmings are especially well adapted for such activity as they grow large claws

BROWN LEMMING (left)	ᐊᕝᓐᖅ	Avinngaq	*Lemmus trimucronatus*
	ᑲᔪᖅᑕᖅ	Kajuqtaq	
COLLARED LEMMING (right, in winter coat)	ᐊᕝᓐᖅ	Avinngaq	*Discrostonyx groenlandicus*
In winter	ᐊᒥᕐᑕ	Amirta	
	ᕿᓚᖕᒥᐅᑕᖅ	Qilangmiutaq	

on their forefeet for burrowing through drifts.

Lemmings are extremely prolific breeders, sometimes having a litter as often as every 3 to 4 weeks. In some years they breed all year round with a pause during spring and fall, while at other times, in response to population abundance, they may not breed in winter.

Lemming populations undergo dramatic peaks and crashes, thought to be influenced by weather and possibly behavioural factors. In a mild winter, with an abundance of food such as buds, bark, and willow twigs, populations may reach peaks of 50-100 lemmings per hectare of tundra. In low years, only a single lemming may be found over 4-6 hectares.

When lemmings are abundant their predators thrive also. Ermine, arctic foxes, wolves, wolverines, owls, hawks, falcons, gulls, and jaegers all feed on lemmings and the numbers of several of those species fluctuate with the lemming populations.

Beaver and muskrat are members of the rodent order and are adapted to an aquatic way of life. Although characteristically associated with areas

| **BEAVER**
(top) | ᐱᒋᐊᖅ | Kigiaq | *Castor canadensis* |
| **MUSKRAT**
(bottom) | ᐊᕕᓐᖔᕐᔪᐊᖅ | Avinngarjuaq | *Ondatra zibethica* |

19

below the treeline, both species are occasionally found in river systems on the barren-grounds. When present, beaver are most likely to be found in locations where willows grow in thickets, while muskrat require only marshy or delta areas.

Both species are well-known for the dwellings they construct, but on the barrens they usually occupy dens in riverbanks rather than lodges or houses. The living sites must be chosen with care. If the water body is too shallow, it may freeze to the bottom in winter and the animals will perish. Both species are active beneath the ice all winter.

The beaver is large for a rodent, averaging about 20 kg in weight, while the muskrat is much smaller, weighing about 1.5 kg. Both have scaly hairless tails. That of the beaver is broad and flat, shaped like a paddle, while that of the muskrat is narrow like an oar.

Beaver and muskrat live in family units, but where beaver work together co-operatively, muskrat tend to be quarrelsome. The young of both species are called kits.

BLUE WHALE

The blue whale, which may reach a length of 30 m and weigh in excess of 100 tonnes, is the largest animal which has ever lived. It is named for its colour, which is slatey blue overlain with pale spots. It has a tiny fin on its back near the rear, and rather small flippers relative to its size.

Blue whales belong to a family of whales called "rorquals". They are distinguished from right whales by a series of grooves which extend along the lower jaw, throat and chest, allowing the whale to expand its jaws when feeding. Rorquals have short flat heads and streamlined bodies.

The blue whale has up to 400 black baleen plates suspended from its upper jaw. When the whale opens its mouth, it takes in seawater and planktonic crustaceans or "krill". When the mouth is closed again, the water is forced out between the baleen plates, and the krill, which are filtered through the fringes of the plates, are swallowed.

Blue whales are found in both the Atlantic and Pacific Oceans. In the summer they move into arctic and antarctic waters. The northernmost limit of their range in Canadian waters is Davis Strait. They are either solitary or occur in small groups of three or four. They can swim rapidly at 10-15 knots and can make up to 20 short shallow dives followed by a deep dive lasting about half-an-hour.

Blue whales are thought to be extremely long-lived and age estimates of 30 to 100 years have been suggested. However, as a result of excessive hunting, their numbers have declined from a world population of over 100,000 to a few thousand. They are now considered an endangered species.

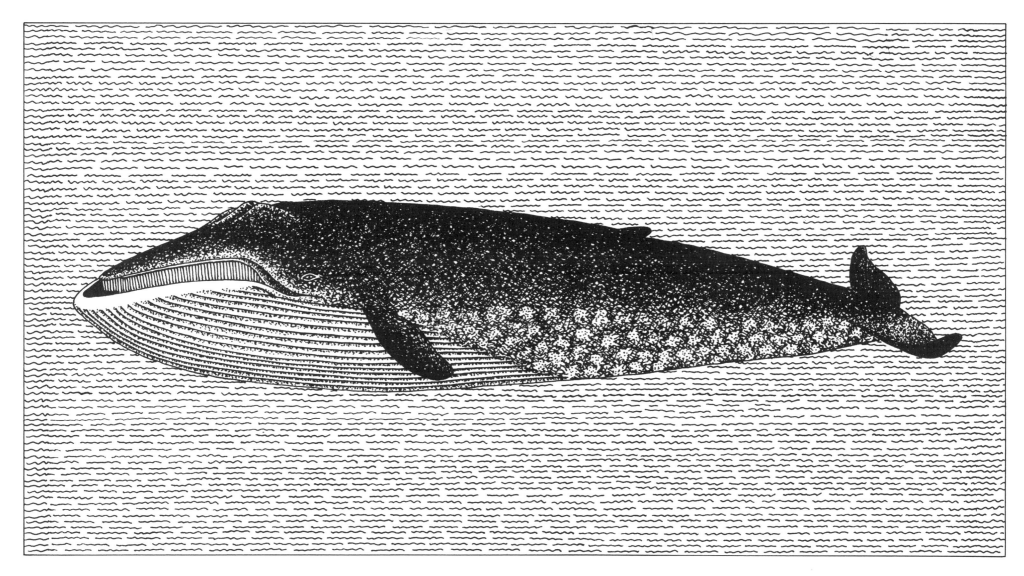

BLUE WHALE   △< ᵇ   Ipak   *Balaenoptera musculus*

BOWHEAD

BOWHEAD ⊲ˢ∧ᵇ Arvik *Balaena mysticetus*

Bowheads belong to the right whale family, which received its name in early whaling days. Being slow swimmers and floating (rather than sinking) when killed, as well as providing a large amount of oil, they were the "right" whales to hunt.

Right whales have very large heads compared to their body size. Inside their mouths are numerous baleen plates or "whalebone" which are used to filter from the sea small planktonic crustaceans, or "krill", which is their main food. Bowheads may grow up to 20 m long and weigh about 50 tonnes. They are dark black or bluish-grey with a pale throat and underbelly.

The bowhead is the only species of baleen whale to inhabit polar waters year round. In summer they are found in Lancaster Sound, Davis Strait and northern Hudson Bay. They winter in the loose ice or open water of Davis Strait, off the west coast of Greenland, and may venture as far south as northern Labrador. They are not restricted to ice-free areas as they can use their heads and bodies to push through half-a-meter or more of solid ice.

Little is known of bowhead whale reproduction. It is thought that mating occurs from February to March and gestation takes about 10-12 months. Usually a single calf is born. Calves may be up to 4.5 m long at birth. They nurse for about a year during which time they grow about 3 m.

Bowheads have been hunted commercially in arctic waters since the 17th century and have rapidly declined in numbers. Today they are listed as an endangered species and can no longer be hunted in Canada.

The shape of sperm whales is well known, for this is the characteristic outline used in popular depictions of whales. They are the largest of all toothed whales, with the largest ones growing over 15 m in length and weighing in excess of 50 tonnes. The enormous head takes up about one-third of the body length and the lower jaw is small and short in comparison. Their teeth grow up to 20 cm long, enabling them to feed on marine life such as fish, sharks, squid, and octopus. Sperm whales are slate grey or almost black, slightly paler underneath, and become lighter with age. Albinos, such as the legendary Moby Dick, have been observed.

Sperm whales are migratory, but only bulls travel to arctic waters, where in summer months they are found in Davis Strait off the coast of Baffin Island. They dive to great depths — some have been captured as deep as 3 km — and remain submerged for as long as 80 minutes. Their principal food is squid.

The sperm whaling industry had its heyday in the early part of the 19th century after which it slowly declined. Sperm whales were hunted for meat, blubber, spermaceti and ambergris. Spermaceti is a clear, colourless oil from a cavity in the head of the whale, and ambergris is a waxy substance found in the large intestine and rectum.

During the peak years of the sperm whaling industry, over 30,000 animals were killed annually. Today, the International Whaling Commission, which was established in the late 1940's to regulate and conserve whale stocks, sets annual quotas for sperm and other whales.

SPERM WHALE   ᑭᒍᑎᓕᒃ   Kigutilik   *Physeter catodon*

NARWHAL

The narwhal is sometimes called the unicorn of the sea because of the long spiral tusk which projects through the upper lip of the male. In the female, the tooth usually remains embedded in the gum, but occasionally a short tusk may form. Narwhal grow to a length of 5 m and can weigh over 1 tonne. Young narwhal are liver-brown at birth. They then turn bluish-grey and become paler as they grow older.

Narwhal are sociable creatures generally forming groups of about 10 individuals, although sometimes during migration herds of a thousand or more are seen. Narwhal feed on fish, squid, octopus and molluscs. To catch their prey, they may sometimes dive to about 200 fathoms, then return to the surface to breathe before diving again.

Narwhal are found throughout the eastern arctic, migrating with the ice in spring and fall. In winter they are known in Davis Strait and Baffin Bay, and in spring move westward through Lancaster Sound and presumably Hudson Strait. In summer they are seen in Jones, Lancaster and Eclipse Sounds, in Admiralty and Prince Regent Inlets, and to a lesser extent in northern Hudson Bay and Foxe Basin.

NARWHAL	ᑐᒑᓕᒃ	Tuugaalik	*Monodon monoceros*
	ᕿᕐᓂᖅᑕᖅ ᕿᓚᓗᒐᖅ	Qirniqtaq qilalugaq	
	ᐊᓪᓚᖑᐊᖅ	Allanguaq	
Female	ᐊᕐᓇᓪᓗᐊᖅ	Arnalluaq	
	ᐊᕐᓇᓪᓗᖅ	Arnalluq	

Sometimes in early winter a group of narwhal may become trapped by ice in straits or fiords. Unless the ice moves out again, or the animals find a series of breathing holes which enable them to escape, their chances for survival are slim.

Narwhal have always been highly valued by Inuit. Traditionally they provided oil for use in lamps and their hides were used for covering whale boats and for boot soles. Today narwhal are hunted under a quota system which in 1983 permitted Inuit communities in the Northwest Territories a total of 542 animals. The tusks are sold to local stores and sometimes to tourists for fairly substantial sums of money. Each animal (or tusk) must have a tag attached to prove it was legally taken.

Belugas, or white whales, resemble a tuskless narwhal. Both these small arctic whales are believed to be primitive dolphins. Belugas live primarily in arctic waters, but there is a small population in the Gulf of St. Lawrence and wanderers have been sighted in the Bay of Fundy. Belugas have also been observed several hundred kilometers up large arctic rivers, although usually they remain near the estuaries.

BELUGA ᕿᓇᓗᒐᖅ Qinalugaq *Delphinapterus leucas*
ᕿᓚᓗᒐᖅ Qilalugaq
ᖃᐅᓗᖅᑕᖅ Qauluqtaq
Immature whale ᐃᔅᓱᖅᑲᖅ Issuqqaq

Belugas are usually found in small groups of up to 12 animals, except during migrations when herds of several hundred travel to shallow coastal waters in summer, and return to deep open water when the bays freeze over in fall.

Spring is the mating season for belugas, and one calf is born in the following spring or summer, about once every three years. The young are between 1 and 1.5 m long. At birth they are a dark slate colour which lightens to grey, and finally turns white when the calf is 4 or 5 years old and about 3 m long. Male belugas can eventually attain a length of 4-6 m and females 4 m.

Belugas feed mainly on fish, supplemented by invertebrates, such as squid and shrimp. Their predators are killer whales and man. Inuit traditionally used the skins to cover their boats ("umiaks") and also ate it, raw or cooked, as "muktuk". The oil was used for lamps.

Commercial operations used to exist at Churchill, Whale Cove and Pangnirtung, before commercial whaling was banned by the Canadian government in 1972.

KILLER WHALE

The killer whale actually belongs to the dolphin family of which it is the largest member. Adult males may grow to a length of 9 m and weigh over 8 tonnes. Females are somewhat smaller and have a much smaller dorsal fin than males. The male dorsal fin extends nearly 2 m above the back. Both sexes have handsomely marked, streamlined bodies, which are shiny black above and white below.

Killer whales are found throughout the oceans of the world. In arctic waters they occur in Foxe Basin, Hudson Bay, Hudson and Davis Straits, Lancaster and Eclipse Sounds, and Admiralty Inlet. In the west the killer whale is found occasionally in the Beaufort Sea.

Killer whales are thought to have two distinct lifestyles, depending on the area they inhabit. Those on the west coast form resident pods which are highly sociable, cohesive groups inhabiting a specific home range. Whales in arctic waters, particularly in the east, probably tend towards a nomadic lifestyle, travelling either singly or in small groups and appearing unpredictably and sporadically in different areas.

Killer whales are carnivores and prey on fishes, birds, seals and whales. They hunt in both deep and shallow water and have been observed pursuing sea lions right up on shore.

Little is known of the mating habits of killer whales other than that there is probably no particular breeding season. The gestation period is thought to be about 16 months and usually only a single calf, 2-3 m long, is born.

Killer whales were not important to early whalers, but they have been hunted to some extent, especially by the Japanese. Despite their reputation for rapaciousness, many have been tamed in aquariums where they perform jumping and retrieving tricks. They are not hunted in the Canadian arctic, although they may be fired upon when seen, more out of fear than need. They sometimes drive narwhal, beluga, and seals close to shore where they can be more easily killed by hunters.

KILLER WHALE ᐋᕐᓗᖅ Aarluq *Orcinus orca*
ᐋᕐᓗ Aarlu

BEARDED SEAL

This seal, known as the square flipper, is one of the largest seals in Canadian waters, averaging 2.5 m in length and 270 kg in weight. It has a coat of stiff grey hairs and a dark brown head. An annual moult occurs between March and June. As its name suggests, the bearded seal has a conspicuous set of whiskers.

Bearded seals spend most of their time in shallow water where they feed on crustacea, molluscs and bottom-feeding fish. In Canada, bearded seals are found in all arctic waters which form pack ice in winter but are generally open in summer. They also occur far up estuaries and bays such as Wager Bay and sometimes in inland lakes in the Keewatin.

Bearded seals are not particularly gregarious animals and prefer pairs or small groups instead of large herds. Mating usually occurs in mid-May and pups are born the following April or May. Females give birth only once every 2 years.

The pups are large and weigh up to 40 kg. They develop rather slowly and remain with their mothers for an extended period of time. By the time they are 6 or 7 years old, both males and females have reached sexual maturity.

Bearded seals are hunted by the Inuit for their hides and for food for themselves and their dogs. Being exceptionally tough and durable, the hides are also prized for use as kamik soles, harpoon lines and dog traces.

RINGED SEAL

Ringed seals are the most common northern seal. They occur throughout arctic and subarctic waters as far south as the Gulf of St. Lawrence. They prefer land-fast ice or solid ice but may also be seen on the floes of the open sea.

They are the smallest of the seal family and average 68 kg in weight and less than 1.5 m in length. Adult ringed seals are white to creamy yellow underneath, and brown to bluish-black on top with irregular cream-coloured rings with dark centres. The young are called "white-coats" because their fur for about 1 month after birth is soft and pure white.

Pups are born in snow dens between mid-March and mid-April on land-fast ice where they remain and nurse for about 2 months. As the ice breaks up in early summer, they take to the water learning to swim and hunt. Adults are mostly sedentary at this time, fasting and basking on the ice, scratching off their old pelts with hind flippers as they undergo an annual moult.

Ringed seals feed primarily upon shrimp-like crustaceans and polar cod. They themselves are the main food of polar bears, which stalk the basking seals on the ice in summer, or kill them with a single blow to the head as they surface at breathing holes in winter. In the water, seals are preyed upon by sharks and killer whales. Pups are often hunted in their dens by arctic foxes and polar bears.

The ringed seal is the most economically important of all seals to coastal Inuit. Traditionally, most parts of the seal were used. The intestines were made into containers and igloo windows, the fat was burned for light and heat, the skins became parkas, mukluks, tents and mats, and the bones were fashioned into tools. Today, ringed seals are hunted primarily for their pelts and meat.

BEARDED SEAL (left)	ᐅᒡᔪᒃ	Ugjuk	*Erignathus barbatus*
Pup	ᑎᕆᒡᓗᒃ	Tirigluk	
	ᑎᕆᒡᓛᖅ	Tiriglaaq	
	ᐅᒡᔪᒐᓛᖅ	Ugjugalaaq	

RINGED SEAL	ᐊᓯᕐᖅ	Natsiq	*Phoca hispida*	Female with pup	ᐊᓯᕐᐊᓴᓐᑉ /	Natsialik / Nattialik
(right)	ᐊᓯᑎᖅ	Nattiq			ᐊᓯᑎᐊᓴᓐᑉ	
Newborn pup				Female without pup	ᖑᓂᖅ	Nuniq
(whitecoat)	ᒥᖅᑯᖅᑐᓕᐟ	Miqquqtulik		Bull	ᑎᒡᒐᖅ	Tiggaq
After first moult	ᐊᓯᕐᐊᖅ /ᐊᓯᑎᐊᖅ	Natsiaq / Nattiaq		Seal in summer fur	ᒥᖅᕿᐊᖅ	Miqqiaq
Pups when crawling				Seal when moulting	ᒪᒪᐊᖅᑐᖅ	Mamaaqtuq
on ice	ᐸᐋᖕᒍᓕᐊᖅ	Paannguliaq		Dwarf seal	ᐊᔭᓇᖅ	Najanaq
First summer, male or						
female	ᐊᓯᕐᐊᐱᓂᖅ /	Natsiaviniq /				
	ᐊᓯᑎᐊᐱᓂᖅ	Nattiaviniq				
Yearling, male or						
female	ᐱᐱᓂᖅ	Piviniq				

HARP SEAL

Harp seals are named for the black harp-shaped saddle which on males runs along each side and over the shoulders. The harp is less clearly defined on the female. The rest of the body is pale grey and the head is black. Harp seals are slightly larger than ringed and harbour seals, averaging 1.7 m in length and 135 kg in weight.

In the arctic, harp seals are found mostly in eastern waters where they range throughout Foxe Basin, the north and east part of Hudson Bay, Hudson and Davis Straits, and the northernmost limits of Baffin Bay during the summer.

Harp seals are migratory, following the melting ice northward in late May and spending the summer in arctic waters. When the ice forms in fall they return south to winter in the Gulf of St. Lawrence and off the Newfoundland coast. In February or March when those waters freeze over, the seals haul out on the edge of the pack ice to give birth to their pups and to mate about a week later.

The newborn pups are called "whitecoats" because of their pure white, long fluffy coats. Within 2 weeks these coats are shed and replaced by short grey ones, which later become creamy brown with dark blotches. When they are about 1 month old, the pups take to the water where they learn to swim, dive and catch fish, without the benefit of their mothers who have abandoned them a few weeks after birth.

In the past, when seals were the mainstay of life for many Inuit, all parts were used for food, boots, clothing, oil and dog food. Today, harp seals are hunted primarily for meat.

HARBOUR SEAL

Although harbour seals are the most widespread and best known seals in other parts of the world, they are not common in the Northwest Territories and occur only in the shallow coastal waters of Hudson Bay, off the shores of Baffin Island, and in Hudson and Davis Straits.

Harbour seals average about 1.5 m in length and weigh about 70 kg. Mature males are slightly larger than females. Although colour is variable, most animals are pale grey and covered with dark spots or blotches. The underside is creamy with dark brown spots. Some individuals may look almost black because of an abundance of spots. Harbour seals moult in late summer and early fall.

The diet of harbour seals is mainly fish. When not feeding, they are sedentary and spend a great deal of time on land, hauling out at low tide. They are often found far up harbours, coastal rivers, and bays such as Chesterfield Inlet and Wager Bay.

Harbour seals often rest together in large groups, but these herds are largely unstructured and impermanent. Mating occurs during late summer and early fall. Pups are born the following May or June, usually on land, but sometimes in the water if stormy weather or predators are present.

Seal pups can swim when they are born, and dive within a few days. They develop quickly and are weaned in a month. By the time they are a year old, they have tripled in weight to about 27-40 kg.

Predators of all seals in northern waters include polar bears, walrus, killer whales and man. Harbour seals are among those which Inuit hunt for hides and food. However, in the north they are not pursued as vigorously as on the Pacific and Atlantic coasts where bounties have been paid and where there is a strong commercial market for pelts.

HOODED SEAL

Hooded seals are also known as bladdernose seals. Males have an inflatable pouch which usually hangs limp and wrinkled over the nose. For mating display the pouch may be blown up to twice the size of a soccer ball. Hooded seals also have an inflatable membrane which can extrude, like a bright red balloon, from one nostril.

Hooded seals are our largest seals. Males average between 2 and 3 m in length and weigh up to 450 kg. Females are slightly smaller. Males are

HARP SEAL (top left)	ᖃᐃ ᕈᓕᒃ	Qairulik	*Phoca groenlandica*
HARBOUR SEAL (centre)	ᖃᓯᒋᐊᖅ	Qasigiaq	*Phoca vitulina*
HOODED SEAL (bottom left)	ᓇᑦᓯᕙᒃ ᐊᐸ	Natsivak Apa	*Cystophora cristata*

darker in colour than females, but both have bluish-grey coats with irregular dark brown spots and blotches. Pups, called "bluebacks", are born slate blue with darker heads. Before birth they shed the white coat common to other seal species.

In the Northwest Territories, hooded seals range throughout the waters of Foxe Basin, northeast Hudson Bay, Hudson Strait, Davis Strait, and northernmost Baffin Island.

With the exception of their cohabitation during breeding season, hooded seals lead solitary lives. In early spring, they are found hauled out on the pack ice off the northern coast of Newfoundland where they gather for breeding. During that time, they form family groups consisting of a female with her newborn pup and an attentive bull who helps the female defend the pup. After a few weeks the pair mates and both desert the pup to return to the sea.

The seals begin to migrate north in April cutting across Davis Strait towards Greenland. A few continue up the west coast of Greenland but most migrate around to the east coast and congregate to moult on the pack ice in Denmark Strait. In late August and early September they return south.

WALRUS

The walrus's family name *Odobenidae* means "those that walk with their teeth." Although not literally true, walrus do in fact use their enlarged canines for many activities, including hauling themselves across ice and up the sides of floes. Both sexes have tusks, which in males can grow up to 1 m in length (though they rarely exceed 60 cm) and weigh over 4.5 kg. Female tusks are smaller. The tusks are used as weapons against bears, boats, and other walrus, as indicators of superiority in males, and for manoeuvering young pups about. Contrary to popular belief walrus do not use their tusks to plough the ocean floor for food.

Walrus rarely dive deeper than 75 m to locate their food which consists of molluscs and invertebrates. They must therefore remain close to shallow coastal waters, undertaking local migrations when solid ice forms in winter.

After feeding, walrus haul out on ice floes and rocky promontories to relax in densely packed groups, jockeying for position and resting their tusks on a neighbour's back. Their senses do not seem very acute and early hunters reported being able to easily approach groups of sleeping walruses and shoot one or two before the others took flight. However, extensive hunting since the 17th century has made walrus wary of man and also caused them to abandon some traditional ranges and hauling-out spots. Whereas the Atlantic walrus *(O.r. rosmarus)* was once found as far south as the Bay of Fundy and the Magdalen Islands in the Gulf of St. Lawrence, its range in Canada is now restricted mainly to Hudson Bay, the waters surrounding Baffin Island, and the high arctic. The Pacific walrus *(O.r. divergens)* is rarely sighted in the Canadian Beaufort.

WALRUS	ᐊᐃᕕᖅ	Aiviq	*Odobenus rosmarus*
Pup	ᐊᐃᕕᐊᓛᖅ/ᐃᓴᐅᒐᖅ/ ᓄᑲᑐᒐᕐᔪᐊᖅ	Aivialaaq / Isaugaq / Nukatugarjuaq	
Adolescent male	ᓄᑲᑐᒐᖅ	Nukatugaq	
Big bull (leader)	ᑎᖕᒥᖅᑎ ᐅᕕᖕᒋᐊᔪᖅ ᕿᕐᓇᓗᒃ	Tingmiqti/Timmiqti Uvingiajuq Qirnaluk	

Shrews	masked shrew	*Sorex cinereus*
	arctic shrew	*Sorex arcticus*
Hares	arctic hare	*Lepus arcticus*
Rodents	arctic ground squirrel	*Spermophilus parryii*
	northern red-backed vole	*Clethrionomys rutilus*
	meadow vole	*Microtus pennsylvannicus*
	root vole	*Microtus oeconomus*
	brown lemming	*Lemmus sibiricus*
	collared lemming	*Dicrostonyx torquatus*
Carnivores	wolf	*Canis lupus*
	arctic fox	*Alopex lagopus*
	red fox	*Vulpes vulpes*
	grizzly bear	*Ursus arctos*
	polar bear	*Ursus maritimus*
	ermine	*Mustela erminea*
	wolverine	*Gulo gulo*
	lynx	*Lynx lynx*
Hoofed Animals	caribou	*Rangifer tarandus*
	moose	*Alces alces*
	muskox	*Ovibos moschatus*
Seals	ringed seal	*Phoca hispida*
	bearded seal	*Erignathus barbatus*
	harbour seal	*Phoca vitulina*
	harp seal	*Phoca groenlandica*
	hooded seal	*Cystophora cristata*
	walrus	*Odobenus rosmarus*
Whales	beluga	*Delphinapterus leucas*
	narwhal	*Monodon monoceros*
	killer whale	*Orcinus orca*
	sperm whale	*Physeter catodon*
	white-beaked dolphin	*Lagenorhynchus albirostris*
	Atlantic pilot whale	*Globicephala melaena*
	harbour porpoise	*Phocoena phocoena*
	minke whale	*Balaenoptera acutorostrata*
	blue whale	*Balaenoptera musculus*
	bowhead	*Balaena mysticetus*

BIRDS

Feathers set birds apart from all other animals. Not only do they enable birds to fly, but they also act as an insulating layer which permits the maintenance of a high body temperature. Both characteristics combine to make birds the most mobile of all animals, enabling them to colonize virtually every corner of the globe.

A direct function of this high mobility is migratory behaviour, which in most birds is highly developed. It enables them to move back and forth between areas when food sources are most abundant, and to escape the hardship of winter, which other animals must endure.

Since feathers are so important, all birds replace them at least once a year by moulting old ones and growing new ones. Many species also undergo partial moults in the spring in order to develop special plumages for courtship display. Usually the male is more colourful, while the female is drab and inconspicuous. This difference helps protect the female from predators when she is most vulnerable — when nesting and rearing her young.

Though the Northwest Territories is home to comparatively few species of birds year-round, it hosts immense numbers during the brief explosion of spring and summer. So important is the Northwest Territories as a nesting and brood-raising area that 16 migratory bird sanctuaries have been established, covering 11 million hectares. Most of these are for the protection of waterfowl, since one-fifth of the continental population of all ducks, geese and swans nest in the Northest Territories.

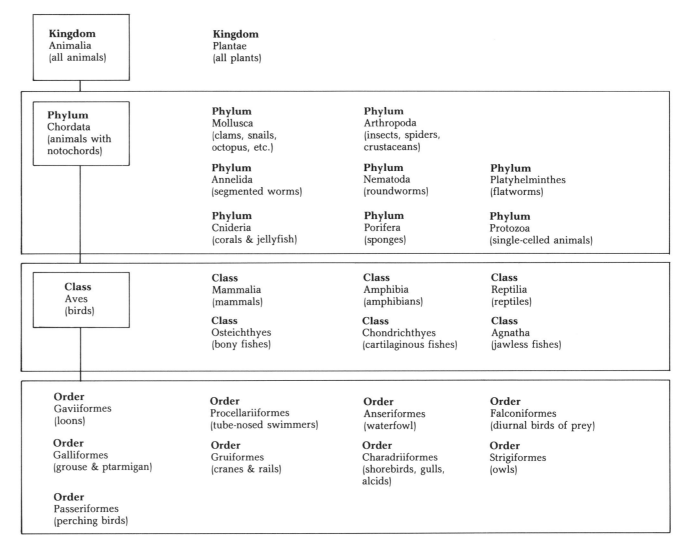

Simplified diagram showing avian orders with representatives found above the treeline in the Northwest Territories, and their relationship to other organisms.

Note: Describing birds can be a tricky business due to the differences in plumage which many species exhibit as a result of age, sex or breeding condition. Since most birds which occur in the Northwest Territories are summer residents only, the following descriptions (sketchy as they are) are limited to the summer plumages of adult males, unless otherwise noted.

Descriptions of the breeding areas in the following pages are generally confined to their occurence above the treeline in the Northwest Territories. Mention of breeding locations outside this area is not usually made.

LOONS

Loons are heavy-bodied birds with strong pointed bills, webbed feet, and short stiff tails. The legs are attached far back on the body, and while this makes loons awkward on land, it facilitates swimming and diving. Loons sit low in the water and dive from the surface. They can remain submerged for several minutes if necessary, and swim very rapidly underwater. Loons are fisheaters, catching their prey in underwater pursuit. When taking off, they must flap and run across the water's surface a lengthy distance before becoming airborne.

Loons are seldom found on land except when nesting. Their nests are built close to the water's edge on freshwater lakes. Usually 2 eggs are laid, their colour olive to brown with darker spots or blotches.

Four species occur in the Northwest Territories: the common loon, the arctic loon, the red-throated loon, and the yellow-billed loon. All are found throughout most of the mainland above the treeline and (except for the yellow-billed loon) on Baffin Island. In addition, all except the common loon are found on a number of arctic islands.

RED-THROATED LOON (top left)	ᖃᖅᓴᐅᖅ	Qaqsauq	*Gavia stellata*
COMMON LOON (bottom left)	ᑐᓕᒡᔪᐊᖅ ᑐᓕᒃ	Tuulligjuaq Tuullik	*Gavia immer*
ARCTIC LOON (bottom right)	ᑲᓗᒃ ᑲᒡᗷᓗᒃ	Kaglulik Kagɬulik	*Gavia arctica*

The common and yellow-billed loons are similar in appearance, the main difference being the shape and colour of the bill (black and yellow-white, respectively). Both have greenish-black heads while the arctic and red-throated loons have grey heads. The red-throated loon is distinguished by a reddish throat patch and the absence of a black-and-white checkered back, which pattern is shared by the other three species. The red-throated loon is also the only loon able to take off from land.

The common loon is most famous for its weird vocalizations, which include yodels and whinnies, as well as the mournful wail which it shares with the other three species.

The tundra swan, which was formerly known as the whistling swan, is one of the largest birds found in the arctic. It has a wingspan of over 200 cm and a weight of 5-8 kg. It is completely white except for a slight rusty stain on the head and neck of some birds. The bill is black with bare skin extending back to the eye and sometimes a yellow or orange spot in front of the eye. The legs are black.

Tundra swans generally arrive in the Northwest Territories by about mid-May. They breed on the mainland

TUNDRA SWAN   ᖁᒡᔪᒃ   Qugjuk   *Cygnus columbianus*

above the treeline, as well as on King William Island and the islands in Hudson Bay, and on parts of Banks, Victoria and Baffin Islands.

Courtship begins in late winter and continues through the spring migration. Although the birds do not breed until after their 4th or 5th year, they may select a mate a year before and lay claim to a territory without actually nesting. Those that do breed begin to nest in late May or early June before the snow melts. The swans are solitary nesters and each pair requires a territory that may be as large as 2 sq. km. The nest is a large mass of vegetation. It is usually located on an island in a pond or small lake so that the birds can feed on shallow-growing aquatic plants.

The number of eggs laid is dependent on the weather. In very cold years the swans may not lay at all, while in a warm spring each nest may contain 5 or 6 eggs. The large, creamy white eggs are incubated only by the female, but the male is always close by, standing guard.

Some eggs are lost to jaegers, wolves, foxes and bears, but usually two adult swans represent a formidable defence against most predators. However, the mortality rate of young swans, or cygnets, is quite high, primarily due to cold and starvation.

Families remain together on the breeding ground during August when the moulting adults are flightless. By early September, and sometimes as late as October, when small lakes are starting to freeze, migration begins. Families migrate together in V-shaped flocks of 20 to 80 birds, flying distances of 500 to 1900 km before stopping at large lakes to rest and feed.

Tundra swans winter on the Pacific and Atlantic coasts of the United States, from Washington to California in the west, and from Maryland to North Carolina in the east.

SNOW GOOSE   ᑲᖑᖅ   Kanguq   *Chen caerulescens*
(white phase)

The snow goose has two colour phases, white and blue, which were once thought to be separate species. In the white form, adults are white with black wingtips. In the blue phase, they are dark grey with a white head.

In the Northwest Territories snow geese breed entirely above the treeline in a variety of locations scattered across the arctic. Some of the more important areas, all of which are protected as sanctuaries, are McConnell River in the Keewatin, the Great Plain of the Koukdjuak on Baffin Island, and Bylot, Southampton and Banks Islands.

Snow geese reach their nesting grounds in late May or early June and immediately begin nest building. Often the ground is still snow-covered and the geese may have difficulty finding enough food during nesting. Precipitation and low temperatures can cause loss of eggs. Predation by foxes, jaegers, and large gulls is also a problem.

The 4-7 eggs hatch in 22-24 days. However, mortality in young birds may be heavy during the first 2 weeks of life when wet cold conditions and predators can still cause havoc. In 42-50 days, the goslings fledge and by late August the whole flock is showing signs of restlessness. As soon as the weather dictates, the geese begin to migrate.

Families travel together and the young remain with their parents all winter. In the spring about 75 % of entire families return to the same breeding grounds. Most young leave when adults, who mate for life, begin nesting, but some stay on in the area of the nest. They begin their own pairing at the end of their second or third winter.

Snow geese winter along the coasts of California, Texas and Mexico, and along the Atlantic coast from New Jersey to South Carolina.

SNOW GOOSE ᑲᕐᕐᔪᒃ Kararjuk *Chen caerulescens*
(blue phase) ᖃᕕᖅ Qaviq

CANADA GOOSE

Although there are many subspecies which vary in size and colour, the Canada goose is always readily identified by its black head, black neck and white chinstrap. It breeds throughout the mainland Northwest Territories, as well as on south Baffin and Southampton Islands and parts of Victoria Island.

Canada geese are the earliest of all waterfowl to nest. They arrive in the north while the land is still snow-covered and begin nesting as soon as nest sites are clear. Although they prefer to nest on the ground near water, they employ a greater diversity of nest sites than all other waterfowl. These include marshes, tundra, islands, cliffs, abandoned nests in trees, haystacks, and the tops of muskrat or beaver houses. Waterfowl managers in the south have encouraged nesting by providing artificial sites such as washtubs, sawn-off wooden barrels, and platforms on poles.

The nest is usually a hollow depression lined with vegetation and down. The 4-5 white eggs are incubated by the female for about 4 weeks while the male stands guard.

One to 2 weeks after the goslings hatch, the adults undergo a moult which leaves them temporarily

flightless. This period lasts about 4 weeks, or about the same length of time it takes the young to reach the flight stage. Canadas without broods to raise often migrate to moulting areas. One such place in the Northwest Territories is the Aberdeen and Beverly Lakes region of the Keewatin. Of the sometimes 30,000 birds moulting there, most are large Canadas from breeding areas 3,000 km to the south. Small Canada geese do not commonly undertake moult migrations.

Canada geese winter mainly throughout the continental U.S.A.

BRANT

The brant is a smaller version of the Canada goose with a shorter neck and no chinstrap — though it does have a few white bars on the neck. It is primarily a saltwater bird, breeding on all the islands of the high arctic, along the northern coast of the mainland, and throughout Foxe Basin.

Though brant often nest in loose colonies, they remain susceptible to predators due to their small size. Therefore, they often nest on small islands. The nest is a circular structure built on the ground out of whatever material is nearby. It is then lined with down. Three to 5 creamy-white eggs are laid at the rate of about one

| CANADA GOOSE | ᓂᕐᓕᖅ | Nirliq | *Branta canadensis* |
| | ᐅᓗᐊᒍᓪᓕᒃ | Ulluagullik | |

42

per day and the incubation, by the female only, takes from 22 to 26 days. After about 40 days, the young fledge. By then the short arctic summer is nearly over and migration must start immediately. If winter is exceptionally early, late fledglings may be frozen into the ice on the breeding ground.

During migration, the family units stay together and it is not until the geese return on their spring migration that the young are driven off. Geese mate for life and the adult pair returns to the same area to breed again. The young may return to the breeding grounds but do not mate until the end of their second or third winter.

Brant geese winter as far south as Massachusetts and North Carolina on the east coast and as far as Mexico on the west coast.

Above the treeline, this duck is found only in the southeastern portion of Baffin Island and northeastern Labrador, where it frequents swift rushing rivers and streams.

The adult male is one of the most distinctive of all ducks, with its highly coloured and bizarre markings. Bluish overall with chestnut sides, it has a striking variety of white markings on its head, neck and body. Females, however, are a dull brown.

Harlequins build a down-filled nest on the ground often hidden in long grass, bushes, or amongst boulders. Six or 7 creamy to buff coloured eggs are laid in early summer and the young hatch in about one month. They learn to swim and dive quickly and soon are negotiating rapids and swiftly-flowing water with ease. Both male and female young resemble adult females; males do not develop their distinctive plumage until the second year.

In early fall, the ducks migrate to spend the winter along the coast of southern Labrador, Newfoundland and the Maritimes. In the west they winter along the coast of British Columbia.

BRANT   ᓂᕐᓕᕐᓇᖅ   Nirlirnaq   *Branta bernicla*
ᓂᕐᓕᕐᓇᕐᔪᒃ   Nirlirnaarjuk

HARLEQUIN DUCK   ᑐᓚᔪᓄᒃ   Tulajunuk   *Histrionicus histrionicus*

Pintails are slim agile ducks with long narrow wings. Males can be identified by their long black tail feathers, brown head, and white breast, which continues up the front of the neck and ends in a narrow white stripe on each side of the head. Females are a nondescript mottled brown.

In North America pintails are the most widely distributed duck and the 2nd or 3rd most abundant. In the Northwest Territories they are found throughout the mainland except in the northeastern part of the Keewatin. They reach Yellowknife by the end of April or early May, but may not arrive in places farther north until June. They are more numerous in the western part of their range, with the largest concentration of breeding pairs in the Canadian arctic being found in the Mackenzie Delta.

Pintails are dabbling ducks, which means that they are generally found in ponds, small lakes, and shallow freshwater marshes, where they dip and bob for underwater vegetation. They nest on the ground, usually near water. The nests may be concealed or exposed. Seven to 10 pale olive or buff eggs are laid between the beginning of June and the beginning of July. Incubation requires about 24 days.

PINTAIL   ᖃᒻᒧᐊᔪᐅᖅ   Qummuajuuq   *Anas acuta*
             ᖃᒻᒧᐊᕐᔪᒃ   Qummuarjuk
             ᐊᕐᓇᕕᐊᖅ   Arnaviaq

(male in flight and lower left, female right)

Most pintails winter in California, with most of the remainder going farther south to Mexico. Pairing generally takes place there during late fall and early winter. The male then accompanies his new mate to her breeding area. Thus the entire pintail population undergoes steady mixing and the species remains uniform everywhere.

The male oldsquaw is unique in that it wears two distinct bright plumages, one in winter and one in summer. In the Northwest Territories look for a white eyepatch on a brown head and two long slender tail feathers. The female is similar, but lacks the bold pattern of the male and the long tail feathers.

Pairs arrive at their nesting sites in June. They breed throughout the mainland Northwest Territories and on all arctic islands. Although referred to as a sea duck, the oldsquaw does not restrict itself to nesting along coastlines, but is found widely dispersed across the tundra. However, a small number of breeding birds as well as most juveniles remain in the boreal forest during the summer.

Nests are usually placed near shores of tundra ponds or on islands near the water's edge — often in close associa-

tion with colonies of arctic terns. This affords the oldsquaw a measure of protection against predators, since terns are quick to defend their nests when danger approaches.

An average of 7 eggs is laid, with the incubation period being about 26 days. About 24 hours after hatching, the young are led to water. Sometimes broods combine, resulting in large rafts of ducklings. After several weeks the birds begin making their way to the sea, where they join the males which have preceded them from the nesting grounds. There the flocks increase in size until their departure in September.

Oldsquaws feed primarily on crustaceans, for which they dive deeper than any other duck. Some have been caught at depths of 60 m in the nets of fishermen. Except when migrating, they fly low over the water in irregular flocks, twisting and turning. They are noisy and garrulous at all seasons. They winter along the Atlantic and Pacific coasts, and on the Great Lakes.

OLDSQUAW ◁ᑉᒋˢᵇ Aggiq *Clangula hyemalis*
ᐊᑉᒋᐊˢᒧᑉ Aggiarjuk
ᐋᐊᔨˢᵇ Aa'aangiq
ᐊˢᇬᐱᐊˢᵇ Arnaviaq

(male bottom, female top)

COMMON EIDER

The common eider is a sea duck which breeds near salt water and winters along sea coasts. It is especially fond of areas with mussel beds and reefs where it can dive for food such as molluscs and crustaceans. In arctic Canada the breeding range of the common eider covers the coastlines of Hudson Bay and Baffin Island, a number of arctic islands, and the mainland west from Bathurst Inlet.

Like all sea ducks, the common eider is a heavy, rather thick-necked duck. It has a flat bill, which extends back into the forehead nearly as far as the eyes. Plumage is mainly black and white. Females are mottled brown. Down from the female's breast is the finest and warmest of all down. Eiderdown industries operated in several eastern arctic communities during the 1960's, but none exist today.

Common eiders usually nest in colonies in sheltered rocky areas or in depressions in low vegetation. Four to 7 pale green eggs are laid in the down-lined nest and the peak of hatching occurs in mid-July. As soon as the young hatch, the female leads them to the water where they assemble in large rafts with other families.

Common eiders are year-round residents in some arctic locations. They winter from southern Baffin Island southward along the Atlantic coast to the Maritime provinces, and also in Hudson Bay.

COMMON EIDER	ᐊᒪᐅᓕᒡᔪᐊᖅ	Amauligjuaq	*Somateria mollissima*
	ᐊᒪᐅᓕᒃ	Amaulik	
	ᒥᑎᖅ	Mitiq	
	ᐊᒪᐅᓕᒡᔪᐊᕐᐊᕐᓇᓪᓗᖕᐊ	Amauligjuap arnallunga	
	ᐊᒪᐅᓕᒡᔪᐊᕐ ᓄᓕᐊᔮᖕᐊ	Amauligjuap nuliajaanga	
	ᐊᕐᓇᔨᐊᖅ	Arnaviaq	

(male above, female not shown)

Like the common eider, the king eider is principally black and white. The top of its head and back of its neck is a pale bluish-grey, while the bill is red-orange with an orange knob on the forehead. The female is a dull brown and lacks the bright swelling at the base of the bill.

King eiders breed along the mainland coast west from James Bay and on most arctic islands. Unlike common eiders, they do not nest in colonies and prefer freshwater to marine sites. The nest, which may be some distance from the water, is lined with down. The female lays 4 to 7 olive-coloured eggs and covers them with down whenever she leaves the nest. Incubation is solely by the female and the young hatch in about 22 or 23 days. They then group together in large bands with adult females in charge.

Males, meanwhile, have abandoned the nesting sites to gather in enormous flocks at feeding areas, where they moult, and where mussels and crustaceans are plentiful. Females and young follow later, flying in characteristic king eider style — in long lines low over the water. Although king eiders generally avoid flying over land, many birds cross Baffin Island on their way to Greenland in late summer, flying through Pangnirtung and Kingnait Passes. Others winter on open water off Labrador, the Gulf of St. Lawrence and Newfoundland.

KING EIDER	ᖅᐳᖕᒐᓕᒃ	Qingalik	*Somateria spectabilis*
	ᒥᑎᖅ	Mitiq	
	ᖅᐳᖕᒐᓚᖅ	Qingalaaq	
	ᖅᐳᖕᒐᓕᐅᑉ ᐊᕐᓇᓪᓗᖕᒐ	Qingaliup arnallunga	
	ᖅᐳᖕᒐᓕᐅᑉ ᓄᓕᐊᔮᖕᒐ	Qingaliup nuliajaanga	
	ᐊᕐᓇᕕᐊᖅ	Arnaviaq	

(male left, female right)

47

RED-BREASTED MERGANSER

Mergansers are fish-eating ducks with long thin bills, serrated on the sides. The red-breasted merganser is the only species found above the treeline. Its range extends onto the barrens as far north as Bathurst Inlet and Baker Lake. A few breed on the southeast tip of Victoria Island and on south Baffin Island.

Both male and female have a shaggy crest at the back of the head. The male has a greenish-black head set off by a white collar, while females have a reddish-brown head. Feet and bill are red.

Red-breasted mergansers begin to arrive in the Northwest Territories at the end of May. They nest on the ground under bushes or among rocks, usually near large lakes with plenty of fish. Seven to 12 eggs are laid and newly-hatched chicks are generally seen by mid-July.

Red-breasted mergansers probably leave their nesting grounds in early September, but are rather late migrants through their route south. They have been observed in the Churchill area as late as the first week in October and often stay in Alberta until November when the lakes are almost completely frozen over. Red-

RED-BREASTED MERGANSER	ᐸᐃᖅ	Paiq	*Mergus serrator*
	ᓄᔭᕋᓕᒃ	Nujaralik	
	ᑲᔾᔨᖅᑐᖅ	Kajjiqtuq	
	ᐊᕐᓇᕕᐊᖅ	Arnaviaq	

(male left, female right)

breasted mergansers winter along the Atlantic and Pacific coasts of the United States as far south as the Gulf of Mexico and Baja, California.

The peregrine is one of the swiftest birds in the world, able to pursue its prey in high-speed aerial chases of up to 100 km/hr. In the arctic, peregrines prey on birds varying in size from small songbirds to ducks and ptarmigan. The falcon swoops down on the unsuspecting prey at high speed. It kills by snatching the bird in mid-air and gripping it with its talons, or stuns the prey with a blow from its closed fist and then kills it on the ground.

Peregrine falcons breed throughout most of the Northwest Territories on high rocky cliff ledges usually near the sea or some smaller body of water. The nest is often simply a depression or scrape on the ledge with no apparent nesting material, although sometimes peregrines occupy the stick nests of other birds.

When the birds return to the arctic in April or May, usually to the same area they used the year before, they engage in energetic courtship displays, which consist of superb aerial dives accompanied by much screaming. Courting is followed by egg-laying and

an incubation period of 28-29 days in which both birds participate. Nestlings hatch from mid-June to mid-July and remain about 5 weeks in the eyrie.

Peregrine eggs are beautifully coloured with a brown or rusty-brown background, overlain by small vivid blotches or spots of reds and browns. As such, they were highly prized by egg collectors at the turn of the century. Today, although protected from egg raiders, peregrine populations have declined, largely through the contamination of food by DDT and other pesticides. The subspecies, *F.p. tundrius,* which nests above the treeline, is now listed as threatened, while *F.p. anatum,* which nests in the Mackenzie valley, is considered endangered. Possession of a peregrine or its eggs, or tampering with a nest site, is strictly prohibited unless a permit has been issued.

PEREGRINE FALCON   ᑭᒡᒑᕕᐊᕐᔪᒃ ᑲᒃᑲᔪᖅ   Kiggaviarjuk
Kakkajuuq   *Falco peregrinus*

GYRFALCON

The gyrfalcon is the largest and most magnificent of all falcons. White phase birds are primarily white with dark spots and bars on the back and wings. Dark phase birds occur in shades of grey or brownish colours. The white colour phase is most common in the eastern and high arctic; the dark phase is common on Ungava Peninsula and in the western and low arctic.

The gyrfalcon is primarily an arctic species, remaining in the north year-round. It nests above the treeline on the mainland and on all arctic islands. It frequents open country near cliffs or mountains, both inland and on rocky coasts.

Gyrfalcon nesting depends on the availability of food. If food is insufficient, the birds do not nest. Ptarmigan, ground squirrels and hares are the main items in a gyrfalcon's diet. In coastal areas, seabirds as well as ducks and geese are taken, and small perching birds may also fall prey. Other animals which are hunted by gyrfalcons include lemmings and weasels.

Gyrfalcons do not build their own nests, but usually move into the stick nest of another species. The nest is usually high up on an inaccessible cliff ledge, often near water. Over the years the accumulated remains of prey build up around the site, and the area below becomes stained white with excrement and coloured by the bright orange crusts of lichens.

From 2 to 7, but normally 4, eggs are laid at approximately 2-3 day intervals. They are creamy-white, and spotted and blotched with rusty marks. Incubation, performed mainly by the female, takes about 33-35 days and the young birds remain in the nest another 45-47 days after hatching. For about a month after they fledge, the young fly with their parents near the nest site, learning to hunt.

The wintering habits of gyrfalcons are only just beginning to be understood. It is thought that some juvenile birds from northern areas migrate to parts of southern Canada for the winter. The migratory juveniles are called "passage birds". Some adult birds remain near their breeding sites, feeding on over-wintering ptarmigan and hare.

Many people consider gyrfalcons to be the most graceful and skillful of all falcons. They have always been prized by falconers throughout the world for their size and their ability to take large prey. In the past few years, various organizations in the Northwest Territories have negotiated with other countries wishing to obtain the rare and valuable birds. In 1982 two passage birds, a white phase male and a dark phase female, were exported to the United Arab Emirates. In 1983 two white phase birds were exported.

GYRFALCON ᑭᓐᓄᐊᔪᐊᖅ Qinnuajuaq *Falco rusticolus*
ᑭᒡᒐᕕᒃ Kiggavik
ᑭᒡᒐᕕᐊᕐᔪᒃ Kiggaviarjuk
ᖃᑯᖅᑕᖅ Qakuqtaq

Golden eagles are huge birds with a wingspan of up to 2.5 m. Adults are dark brown with golden-tipped feathers on the crown and nape. Immatures are similar but have much white on the base of the tail and wings. Mature bald eagles can be distinguished from golden eagles by the pure white head and tail of the former, but this plumage does not appear until they are about four years old.

Golden eagles have been observed in various places along the northern coast of the mainland and in the Keewatin, but nowhere are they abundant. They nest on cliffs, building very large structures made of sticks and lined with mosses, grasses and leaves. New material is added yearly. Over a number of years golden eagles often use different nests which are short distances apart.

Two eggs are normally laid in late May or June and the incubation period is 43-45 days. The chicks often hatch a few days apart and in many cases the older eaglet will kill its younger nest mate. This, combined with the fact that eagles do not breed until they are at least 5 years old, accounts in part for the scarcity of the species.

Another factor is that farther south, in farming areas, eagles have been harassed and shot by ranchers who believe they prey heavily on livestock. In the north this of course has not occurred, although golden eagles do prey on young caribou calves. Other food items in the north are hares, ground squirrels, birds, fish and carrion.

Golden eagles migrate to southern Canada and the United States for the winter.

The rough-legged hawk is the only arctic hawk whose legs are completely feathered to the base of the toes. It has a broad tail and wings, and flying overhead can be identified by its distinctive black wrist patches. It is most often seen high in the air, soaring in wide circles.

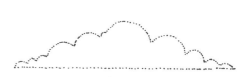

| **ROUGH-LEGGED HAWK** (left) | ᖅᓇᓗᐊᔪᐊᖅ ᑲᔪᖅ | Qinnuajuaq Kaajuuq | *Buteo lagopus* |
| **GOLDEN EAGLE** (right) | ᖁᐸᓗᐊᖅᐸᖅ ᓇᒃᑐᓕᒐᖅ ᓇᒃᑐᕋᓕᒃ | Qupanuaqpaq Naktuligaq Nakturalik | *Aquila chrysaetos* |

51

Rough-legged hawks migrate north between mid-May and mid-June to breed throughout the arctic, from the treeline north to Melville and Prince Patrick Islands, as well as on Baffin and Bylot Islands. They build their nests of twigs and grasses high on cliff ledges, escarpments, large boulders or steep riverbanks. Sometimes several nests are used by the same pair in successive years.

Three or 4 greenish-white eggs streaked with brown are laid soon after the birds arrive, and incubation, lasting 28-31 days, begins immediately. The young remain in the nest until they are about 40 days old, leaving it by early July to mid-August. Southward migration begins about 6 weeks later.

Reproduction by rough-legged hawks varies from year to year because lemmings, which are their main source of food, are cyclic. In a year of low lemming numbers, some birds produce no young.

The rough-legged hawk winters from coast to coast throughout most of the continental U.S.A.

SNOWY OWL

The snowy owl is one of the most spectacular year-round arctic residents. The feathers are sometimes pure white, but more generally they are barred and spotted with dark brown, particularly on the female. The face and throat are white and the beak is almost hidden by the facial feathers. As an adaptation to its arctic environment, the snowy owl has completely feathered legs and toes. Although owls are generally nocturnal, the snowy owl in summer must hunt in broad daylight.

Snowy owls breed throughout most of the Northwest Territories above the treeline, and on all arctic islands. During winter they may be found virtually anywhere throughout the Canadian mainland (except northeastern Keewatin), as well as on the islands in Hudson Bay and on the southern half of Baffin Island.

The snowy owl nests on the open tundra either in a depression on the ground or on top of a large boulder. As many as 9 white eggs are laid and incubation lasts just over a month. Since each egg is laid and hatches at a different time, there is great disparity

SNOWY OWL   ᐅᑉᐱᒍᐊᖅ   Ukpigjuaq   *Nyctea scandiaca*
ᐅᑉᐱᒃ   Ukpik

in the size of the nestlings. Often the younger birds do not survive. Snowy owls are extremely aggressive near their nests and dive at animals or people who approach too closely.

The snowy owl eats rodents and some birds and fish, but its main food item is lemmings. Because lemmings are cyclic, undergoing population crashes every 4 or 5 years, the owls must sometimes wander to unaccustomed areas in search of food. Every few years, therefore, they are seen as far south as the central United States.

The short-eared owl is a medium-sized owl with a brown back, and buffy-yellow head and breast, streaked with brown. Its ear-tufts are small and not usually visible. Unlike most owls, it is active throughout the day, cruising low over open country seeking out voles and lemmings.

Short-eared owls are common during the breeding season in areas such as tundra, marshes, grasslands and low scrub country. They breed throughout the mainland except in the north-eastern part of the Keewatin. Reproductive success likely depends a great deal on the abundance of their

prey species. In years of lemming population crashes, the owls may not breed at all and may even move to other locations where food is more plentiful.

Nests are built on the ground in a shallow depression which is lined with vegetation. The number of eggs, from 4 to 9, depends on the availability of food. The eggs hatch in 24-28 days and the nestlings fledge when they are 31-36 days old.

Short-eared owls leave the Northwest Territories in the fall to spend the winter in southern Canada and much of the United States.

SHORT-EARED OWL   ᐅᓐᓄᐊᖅᓯᐅᑎ   Unnuaqsiuti   *Asio flammeus*

PTARMIGAN

Two species of ptarmigan are found in the Northwest Territories. In winter both are white with black tail feathers. In summer they are brown with white wings and breast.

Though the two species are quite similar in appearance, the willow ptarmigan is a little larger and has a heavier bill. In summer the brown of the willow ptarmigan is more reddish, while that of the rock ptarmigan is paler and more yellowish. In winter rock ptarmigan males have a black line through the eye.

Both species are found throughout the mainland above the treeline. The rock ptarmigan is also found on all arctic islands, while the willow ptarmigan is absent from the most northerly islands and eastern Baffin Island. As its name suggests, the rock ptarmigan frequents higher, more barren hills than the willow ptarmigan. In winter the willow ptarmigan seeks sheltered areas while the rock ptarmigan, which is hardier, does not.

Ptarmigan spend a good deal of their time walking about on the ground — their shuffling tracks in the snow are a common sight everywhere in the north. When approached, their instinct is to remain motionless, hoping to go

WILLOW PTARMIGAN	◁ᖅᐱᒋᕕᖅ	Aqiggiviq	*Lagopus lagopus*
ROCK PTARMIGAN	◁ᖅᐱᒋᖅ	Aqiggiq	*Lagopus mutus*
Ptarmigan in winter plumage (left, in flight)	ᐅᑭᐅᓕᒃ	Ukiulik	
Ptarmigan in summer plumage (right, top and bottom)	◁ᐅᔭᓕᒃ	Aujalik	

unseen, or to scurry away on foot. But if the intruder comes too close they burst into the air and fly off with rapidly beating wings.

In winter they wear a dense mat of feathers on their toes to permit easy movement over soft snow. At night they fly into snowbanks to roost, so that predators may not track them down while they sleep. During the day they feed on the buds and tender leaves of willow and dwarf birch as well as a variety of berries and some insects.

Their mating ritual is similar to other species of grouse and involves males displaying to attract females and to discourage other males. The males develop bright red combs over the eyes. Eggs are laid during June-July, usually half-a-dozen or more. Incubation takes about 3 weeks.

Ptarmigan are year-round residents in the north, though limited migrations southward are sometimes undertaken.

The willow ptarmigan is the state bird of Alaska.

Sandhill cranes are extremely large birds nearly a metre long with a wingspan of up to 2 metres. In flight they can be identified by their outstretched neck, long trailing legs, and characteristic wing stroke (a quick jerk or flap of the wings upwards).

Adults are ash-coloured with a bare red patch on the forehead and crown. The voice is a deep incessant kr-r-r-oo, which sounds a bit like a piece of machinery in need of oiling.

Sandhill cranes may be found throughout most of the arctic, as far north as Banks and Devon Islands. During the breeding season, which may begin in mid to late May, or later, cranes perform an intricate mating dance with stiff legs, outstretched wings and bobbing head. Nests are made on dry tundra ridges near water. Usually 2 buff-coloured eggs, spotted and blotched with brown, are laid. Both parents take part in incubation and the chicks hatch in about a month.

The fall migration begins in early September when the birds fly south to their wintering grounds in the southern United States, central Mexico, and Cuba.

SANDHILL CRANE ᑕᑎᒡᒐᖅ Tatiggaq *Grus canadensis*
ᑕᑎᒡᒐᕐᔪᐊᖅ Tatiggarjuaq

SANDPIPERS

The sandpiper family encompasses a variety of wading birds. Most are coloured brown or grey above, often white below, with long slender legs and short tails. They are often found in flocks in open country at the edge of fresh or salt water — on beaches, mud flats and sandbars. They run rapidly along the shore or wade in shallow water while probing for food with narrow pointed beaks. They fly in close formation with darting aerial symmetry. Many are noted for their long migrations, which take them from the high arctic to South America.

Nests are made in a hollow in the ground, and may be lined with moss, grasses or leaves. Usually 4 eggs are laid. Eggs and chicks are mottled to provide a camouflage effect. The chicks usually leave the nest as soon as their down is dry after hatching. Many begin foraging for themselves immediately, though the adults remain nearby to supervise. Food consists mainly of insects, worms, small crustaceans and molluscs.

Of those members of this family which are found in the Northwest Territories, most breed in tundra areas. These include the whimbrel, Eskimo curlew, Hudsonian godwit, ruddy turnstone, knot, sanderling, dunlin, and long-billed dowitcher; as well as the semipalmated, white-rumped, Baird's pectoral, purple, stilt, and buff-breasted sandpipers.

The common snipe and spotted sandpiper are found just above the treeline in central Keewatin, but their main range extends throughout the interior of Canada. The least sandpiper breeds both above and below the treeline in the Mackenzie and Keewatin regions.

The smallest sandpipers are informally called "peeps" and include the least, white-rumped, Baird's and semipalmated sandpipers. Their name derives from their diminutive size, similar shape and colouration, and from the sound of their calls.

The ruddy turnstone stands apart from other members of this family by its handsome colouration — black and white with orange-red patterns on the wings and back. The pointed upturned bill is adapted for turning over stones to reach worms and crustaceans underneath.

One species, the Eskimo curlew, is now nearly extinct. It was once present in such great numbers that it became a target for market gunners after the depletion (and eventual extinction) of the passenger pigeon. It is similar in appearance to the whimbrel, but smaller.

WHIMBREL ᐱᐊᕐ ᒫᑦᓇᐊᖅ Kiasigaattiaq *Numenius phaeopus*

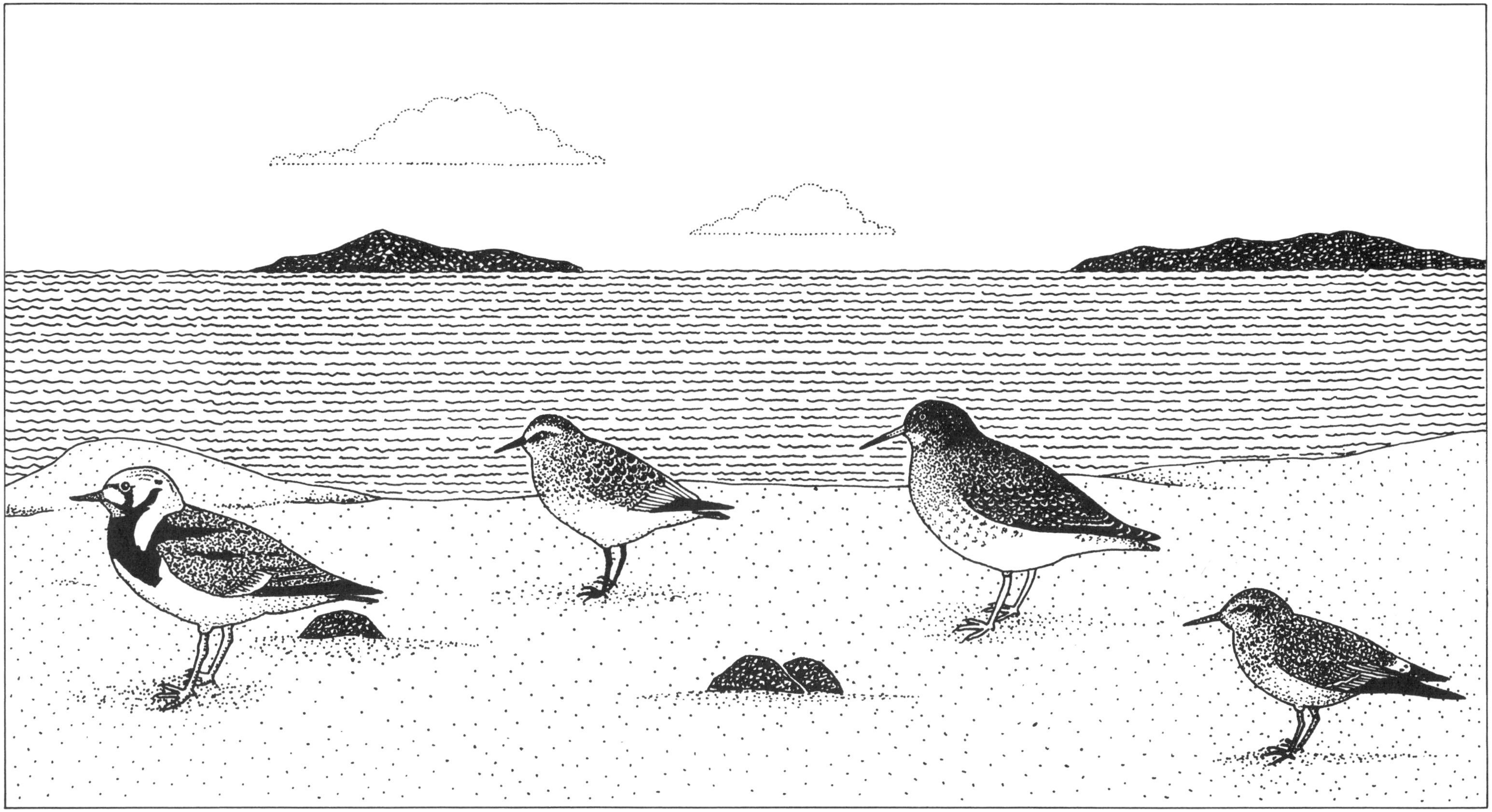

BAIRD'S SANDPIPER (top left)	ᓯᒡᔭᕆᐊᕐᔪᒃ ᑐᐃᑦᓇᖅ ᓕᕕᓕᕕᓛᖅ	Sigjariarjuk Tuitnaq Livilivilaaq	*Calidris bairdii*
RUDDY TURNSTONE (bottom left)	ᑕᓪᓕᕙᖅ	Tallivaq	*Arenaria interpres*
PURPLE SANDPIPER (top right)	ᓯᒡᔭᕆᐊᕐᔪᒃ	Sigjariarjuk	*Calidris maritima*
WHITE-RUMPED SANDPIPER (bottom right)	ᓯᒡᔭᕆᐊᕐᔪᒃ	Sigjariarjuk	*Calidris fuscicollis*

PLOVERS

Plovers are small to medium-sized shorebirds with a plump appearance. In comparison to other waders they have a short neck and short bill. They are most often seen running quickly along the shore, stopping briefly to peck at the ground before continuing on. They forage on insects, worms, small crustaceans and molluscs.

Both sexes are outwardly similar and both incubate the eggs, which are laid in May or June, depending on the species. The eggs, which are usually 4, are cryptically coloured with spots or blotches to make them difficult to see. The nest is a shallow or hollow scrape which may be unlined, or lined sparsely with plant material or other debris. Plovers distract intruders from their nests by feigning injury or sickness and leading them away.

Four species are found above the treeline: ringed, semipalmated, American golden, and black-bellied.

The American golden plover has a black face, throat and breast with a golden spotted back. It breeds on the mainland above the treeline and on the arctic islands as far north as Devon and Melville. Once very abundant before being nearly wiped out by market hunters in the last century, its numbers are now recovering. It under-takes a lengthy migration, wintering in Brazil and Argentina.

The black-bellied plover is similar in appearance to the American golden plover, differing in its larger body size, black and white underparts, and grey spotted back. It is found as far north as the American golden plover, but on the mainland occurs only along parts of the northern coast.

The semipalmated and ringed plovers are nearly identical in appearance, with a white breast and throat, a dark breastband and a grey back. The semipalmated plover is found throughout the mainland and on Banks, Victoria, Southampton and south Baffin Islands. The ringed plover breeds only on Ellesmere, Devon, Bylot and east Baffin Islands.

SEMIPALMATED PLOVER (left)	ᖁᓕᒍᓪᓕᐊᕐᔪᒃ	Qulligulliarjuk	*Charadrius semipalmatus*
	ᖁᓕᖁᓪᓕᐊᖅ	Qulliqulliaq	
AMERICAN GOLDEN PLOVER (right)	ᑐᓪᓕᒃ	Tullik	*Pluvialis dominica*
	ᑐᓪᓕᒑᕐᔪᒃ	Tuulligaarjuk	

Phalaropes are the most aquatic of all shorebirds, sometimes referred to as "swimming sandpipers". They float high in the water, bobbing like a cork, and are noted for their habit of spinning in circles while they feed. They sleep while on water and winter at sea in the southern hemisphere.

Unlike most birds, female phalaropes are larger, more brightly coloured and more aggressive than males. They also initiate courtship. The eggs are incubated by the male alone, who develops brood patches — exposed skin on the abdomen which helps keep the eggs warm. Rearing of the young is also the male's duty.

The northern phalarope is found throughout the mainland above the treeline, and on Victoria, Southampton and south Baffin Islands. It is the most abundant and most widely distributed phalarope, and the one most likely to be seen inland. Females are grey above with a white throat and a reddish patch on the neck.

The red phalarope nests farther north and is more maritime than the northern phalarope. It breeds on a number of arctic islands as far north as Ellesmere, and in eastern Hudson Bay, Foxe Basin, and along portions of the northern coast of the mainland. It is larger than the northern phalarope. The side of the head is white, and its neck, breast and underparts are a uniform reddish colour.

NORTHERN PHALAROPE (left)	ᒋ ᐴ ᖕ ᒡ ᓵ ᐅ ᕐ ᕐ ᖅ	Siggaq Saurraq	*Phalaropus lobatus*
RED PHALAROPE (right)	ᒋ ᐴ ᖕ ᒡ ᓵ ᐅ ᕐ ᕐ ᖅ	Siggaq Saurraq	*Phalaropus fulicaria*

Gulls are a familiar sight to most people. Although there are many species, most have these characteristics in common: a chunky compact body, long pointed wings, soaring flight, and grey and white colours. Many are associated with the ocean and marine coastlines, as is reflected by the name "sea gull" which is often applied indiscriminantly to all gulls. In fact, some species are rarely out of sight of land, and others are broadly distributed throughout the interior of the continent.

Gulls are gregarious. They are nearly always found in flocks or colonies. They are also scavengers and will eat almost anything, including garbage, carrion, small mammals, and the eggs and young of other birds. They have learned how to utilize hard-shelled creatures such as clams and sea urchins by dropping them on rocks from aloft to break them open.

They can drink fresh or salt water. Some species are common around dumps.

Most gulls lay 1 to 3 eggs and nest on the ground or on rocky cliffs. Juvenile plumage is usually a dull brown or grey, and is retained for 1 to 3 years, depending on the species.

The herring gull is probably the best known of all gulls in Canada. Above the treeline it is found on southwest Baffin Island and throughout the mainland, except for the northeastern Keewatin. It has black wingtips, pink legs, and a yellow bill with a red spot on the lower mandible. Thayer's gull is very similar to the herring gull, replacing it in the northeastern Keewatin, north Baffin, and the islands of the high arctic. Its eyes are brown with a fine red eye-ring, whereas the eyes of the herring gull are yellow with a yellow eye-ring. The Iceland gull is a paler version of the herring gull. It is relatively rare, being found only in the south Baffin and northwestern Quebec. It has yellow eyes with a red eye-ring.

The glaucous gull is the largest gull in arctic Canada. It lacks the black wingtips of the herring gull, and has much paler wings and back. It breeds on all arctic islands, the northern coast of the mainland, Southampton Island, and the north, east, and south coasts of Baffin Island. It is rather uncommon and is often seen in flocks of herring gulls. It is more of a predator than other gulls, hunting fish, lemmings, and birds, including alcids, ptarmigan and even small ducks.

The ivory gull is the only gull which is entirely white with black legs. It nests in the high arctic and winters over the drift ice between Baffin Island and Greenland, and south to Newfoundland. Its range is imperfectly known. The species is currently listed as rare.

The black-legged kittiwake is a small gull of the open ocean. Unlike the herring gull, its wingtips are pure black without a dash of white, and its yellow bill has no red spot. In the Northwest Territories it breeds mainly in the region of north Baffin Island.

Sabine's gull breeds on several arctic islands and in Foxe Basin. It is the only gull with a forked tail, and, unlike the other arctic gulls, has a black head.

GLAUCOUS GULL (top left)	ᓇᐅᔭᖅ	Naujaq	*Larus hyperboreus*
	ᓇᐅᔭ	Nauja	
	ᓇᐅᔭᔪᐊᖅ	Naujajjuaq	
	ᑲᐅᒪᐅᒃ	Kaumauk	
IVORY GULL (bottom left)	ᓇᐅᔭᕚᖅ	Naujavaaq	*Pagophila eburnea*
BLACK-LEGGED KITTIWAKE (top right)	ᓇᐅᓗᒃᑐᐊᐱᒃ	Nauluktuapik	*Rissa tridactyla*

HERRING GULL (centre right)	ᓇᐅᔭᖅ	Naujaq	*Larus argentatus*
	ᓇᐅᔭ	Nauja	
	ᓇᐅᔭᔪᐊᖅ	Naujajjuaq	
SABINE'S GULL (bottom centre)	ᐃᖅᑭᕆᐊᕆᐊᔪᒃ	Iqqiriarriarjuk	*Xema sabini*
	ᐃᕿᒡᒐᒋᐊᔪᒃ	Iqiggagiarjuk	

JAEGERS

Jaegers look like dark gulls with elongated central tail feathers. Predatory in nature, they rob nests, hunt rodents (especially lemmings) and other birds (such as the Lapland longspur), and harry gulls and terns, forcing them to disgorge fish which they then devour. They are strong, fast fliers with falconlike wings — pirates of the tundra in summer and of the open ocean in winter.

Three species occur in Canada: long-tailed, parasitic and pomarine (not shown). They may be told apart by their tail feathers. Those of the long-tailed and parasitic jaegers are pointed, 10-20 cm and 6-9 cm in length, respectively. Those of the pomarine jaeger are the same length as the parasitic jaeger, but are blunt and twisted.

The breeding distribution of the parasitic and long-tailed jaegers is very similar. The parasitic jaeger is found throughout the mainland and most of the arctic islands, except the most northerly ones. The long-tailed jaeger is found on all arctic islands and throughout the mainland, though not as far south as the treeline. The pomarine jaeger is limited to south Baffin, Banks, Victoria and a few other islands, and the northwestern coast of the mainland.

Jaegers nest on the tundra. Two eggs are laid and incubated by both sexes. Jaegers winter over the Atlantic and Pacific Oceans, mainly in the southern hemisphere.

LONG-TAILED JAEGER (left)	ᐃᓱᓐᖕᒐᕐᓗᒃ	Isunngarluk	*Stercorarius longicaudus*
	ᐃᓱᓐᖕᒐᖅ	Isunngaq	
	ᑲᒥᒐᓕᒃ	Kamigalik	
PARASITIC JAEGER (right)	ᐃᓱᓐᖕᒐᕐᓗᒃ	Isunngarluk	*Stercorarius parasiticus*
	ᐃᓱᓐᖕᒐᖅ	Isunngaq	

The northern fulmar belongs to a family of birds called shearwaters or tubenoses. It is a sea-going bird which ordinarily comes ashore only to nest. Fulmars resemble gulls in general shape and colouration, but have distinctive tube-like nostrils mounted on a stubby yellow bill. They are also distinguished by their ability to eject a rank-smelling stomach oil when disturbed.

Northern fulmars have a limited distribution in the Northwest Territories, but because of their immense breeding colonies they are very common at sea in the eastern arctic. They nest on the steep cliffs of northern Baffin and nearby islands, laying a single egg on a ledge, either on the bare rock or in a depression in vegetation. Before reaching breeding age, fulmars probably do not come to land until they are 3-4 years old.

Terns are slender birds with long narrow wings, forked tails, and a pointed bill. The arctic tern is grey and white with a black cap and red bill. Though it is primarily a seabird, spending most of its life over the ocean and along the coast, it moves inland during the breeding season and may be found nesting virtually anywhere in the Northwest Territories.

Many birds arrive at nest sites in early June, but do not begin nesting until late June. They are found in colonies and are sometimes joined by waterfowl and other seabirds, which take advantage of the protection offered by the aggressive terns. Nests are usually located near fresh or salt water on tundra, rocky islands, or

NORTHERN FULMAR   ᖃᒃᑯᓘᖅ   Qaqulluq   *Fulmarus glacialis*

ARCTIC TERN   ᐃᒥᖅᑯᑕᐃᓚᖅ   Imiqqutailaq   *Sterna paradisaea*

sand and gravel beaches. One to 3 eggs, buff or olive with dark spots and blotches, are laid. Hatching occurs by the middle or end of July.

Terns are skillful and agile fliers, earning their living by diving into the water in search of small fish. They also undertake spectacular migrations, leaving their breeding grounds in the north to fly to the Antarctic Ocean where they winter for a short time over the pack ice. As daylight hours in the Antarctic decrease, the terns start their return journey up the Atlantic and Pacific coasts following the sun as it returns north.

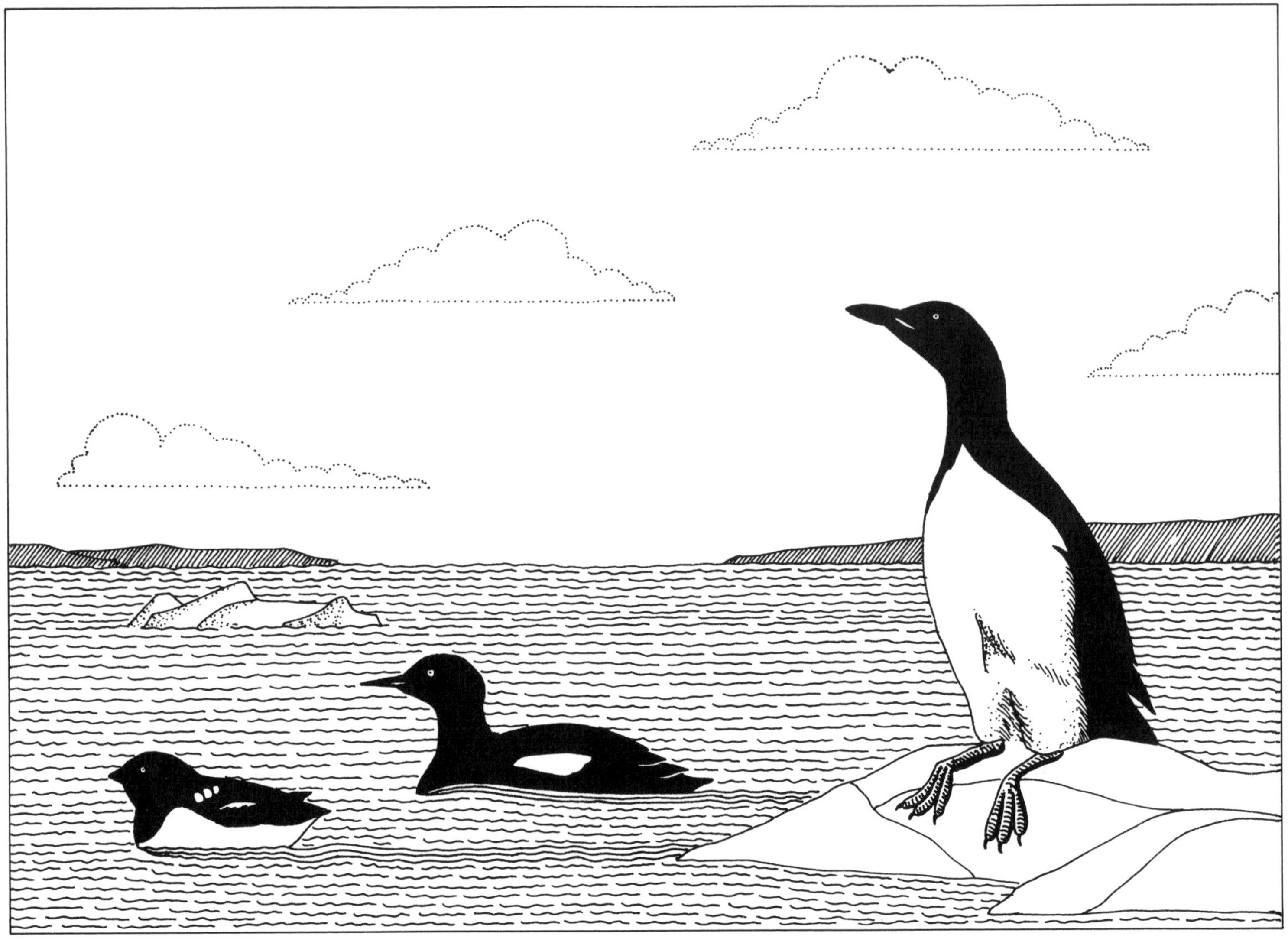

DOVEKIE (left)	ᐊᒃᐸᓕᐊᕐᔪᒃ	Akpaliarjuk	*Alle alle*
BLACK GUILLEMOT (centre)	ᐱᑦᑎᐅᓛᖅ ᐱᑦᓯᐅᓛᖅ	Pittiulaaq Pitsiulaaq	*Cepphus grylle*
THICK-BILLED MURRE (right)	ᐊᒃᐸ	Akpa	*Uria lomvia*

These birds belong to the auk family and are the northern counterparts of penguins — expert swimmers and divers who use their wings to propel themselves underwater. Unlike penguins, however, they have not lost the ability to fly. Their flight is marked by the rapid whirring of wings and a course which is usually set low over the waves. They are gregarious, numbering in the millions, and spend most of their lives at sea. When ashore, they assume a characteristic upright position.

The colour of alcids is predominantly black and white. The tiny dovekie can be recognized by its size (about 20 cm in length), as well as its stubby bill and short thick neck. The black guillemot is all black except for a white wing patch and bright red feet. The largest of the three is the thick-billed murre, which has a white breast that comes to a point at the throat.

The Canadian range of these three species is similar, though not identical, throughout Lancaster Sound, Baffin Bay, Davis Strait, Hudson Strait, and northern Hudson Bay. The thick-billed murre nests in colonies, often immense and crowded, on sea cliffs.

The black guillemot nests in pairs or loose colonies, choosing rocky holes or crevices along the coastline at all elevations. The dovekie is not known to breed in Canada.

The eggs are laid on bare rock — murres 1, guillemots 2. The eggs are pear-shaped, which reduces their likelihood of rolling off cliff ledges; instead, they roll in circles. The chicks of murres leave their nest sites before they are fully fledged, by leaping off cliff ledges which may be hundreds of metres high. Guillemots do not leave the nest until they can fly.

Ravens are the most common year-round birds in many northern communities. They are large black birds with a thick bill, a shaggy ruff at the throat, and a wedge-shaped tail. In flight, they alternately flap and soar like a hawk.

Ravens are said to have great intelligence and tales are told of them outwitting dogs, stealing groceries from the backs of trucks, figuring out garbage can lids, and generally making a nuisance of themselves.

Ravens are found in a variety of habitats but are partial to cliffs and rocky mountainous country where they soar and perform acrobatics on the updrafts. They also congregate in settlements where tall buildings permit the same activities. Garbage dumps too are preferred spots as the raven is a scavenger and carrion-eater. Ravens are often seen in the company of wolves feeding on the remains of caribou on frozen lakes in winter.

Ravens nest on inaccessible cliff ledges in stick nests lined with vegetation, moss, or other soft material. Four to 6 spotted green eggs are laid as early as April in southern locales. The young hatch in about 3 weeks and grow quickly. It is common in July to see parents feeding young ravens almost as large as themselves.

Ravens may be found throughout most of the Northwest Territories but probably do not breed much farther north than the southern part of Ellesmere Island. They generally winter on their breeding range, but some may wander south to join populations in Alberta and Saskatchewan.

RAVEN   ᠊ᠣᠤᠯᕿ   Tulugaq   *Corvus corax*

HORNED LARK

The horned lark is the only lark species native to North America. It is identifiable by its black facial markings and yellow face and throat. The small black horns of the male are not always evident.

Between the middle of May to the middle of June, the horned lark returns to the arctic where it frequents dry places such as eskers, raised beaches, gravel ridges and hilltops. There it walks or runs about, foraging for weed seeds and insects.

The breeding range extends throughout the Keewatin and as far north as Prince Patrick and Devon Islands. The horned lark nests in a dry hollow on the ground where it lays 3 to 5 eggs, which are whitish and speckled with brown. By early June, fledglings appear.

In late August, the larks begin to gather in large flocks and the southward migration is usually underway by the end of September and early October. Horned larks winter in the southern parts of most of the provinces.

LAPLAND LONGSPUR

Early in June, flocks of Lapland longspurs, sometimes consisting of thousands of birds, begin arriving from the south. Males are unmistakable with their black face outlined by a white streak, and a chestnut patch on the back of the neck. Females lack the distinctive black face and are mainly streaked with brown.

Lapland longspurs are among the most abundant and widely distributed small birds in the Northwest Territories. They breed from the treeline north to Ellesmere Island. They nest in wet hummocky tundra, often building the nest in a depression in the ground hidden by surrounding vegetation. Four to 6 greenish-grey eggs, obscured by a darker mottling, are laid sometime between mid-June and mid-July. Incubation is brief, from 10 to 14 days, and by early August the young may be seen running along the ground. At that time they are nearly indistinguishable from the female.

Fall migration begins in September, with the birds moving to wintering grounds in southern Canada and the United States.

WATER PIPIT

The water pipit is a sparrow-sized bird with a slender body and bill. It is a light buffy colour with a streaky breast and sides, and a whitish line over the eyes. The outer tail feathers are lined with white, and the legs are dark brown.

Water pipits are common throughout the mainland above the treeline and on the arctic islands as far north as Baffin, Somerset, Prince of Wales, and Banks Islands.

HORNED LARK (left)	ᖁᐸᓄᐊᕐᔪᒃ	Qupanuarjuk	*Eremophila alpestris*
LAPLAND LONGSPUR (right)	ᕿᕐᓂᖅᑖᖅ	Qirniqtaaq	*Calcarius lapponicus*

Water pipits generally begin arriving in late May. For nesting they prefer dry rocky slopes or alpine meadows. The nest is constructed of grass and twigs and is often hidden under a rock or in low vegetation. Four to 7 white eggs marked with brown are laid and the young hatch quickly, in about 2 weeks. The adults tend the young until early August, feeding them insects found on the edges of puddles and ponds. Water pipits do not hop, but walk along the ground wagging their tails quickly up and down as they feed.

Fall migration begins in late August when large flocks fly south to spend the winter in the United States and Central America.

The common redpoll *(C. flammea)* and hoary redpoll *(C. hornemanni)* are now classed as two distinct species. Yet they are so similar in appearance and habit that some authorities still regard them as one. The main difference between the two is colouration. The common redpoll is noticeably darker and the rump is heavily streaked, whereas the rump of the hoary redpoll is white. Both are small, streaked, buffy-grey and white finches with a crimson cap on the forehead and a tiny black bib under the chin.

Common redpolls are common winter residents in some treed areas of the Northwest Territories. They breed over most of the mainland except along the western Hudson Bay coast and northeastern Keewatin. They also occur on eastern Baffin Island. Hoary redpolls are found breeding on most of the mainland above the treeline as well as on Southampton Island, northern and eastern Baffin Island, and on Devon, Ellesmere, and Axel Heiberg Islands.

In the high arctic, redpolls are generally found in scrubby, rocky tundra. Farther south they prefer spruce and willow thickets.

Nests are constructed on the ground or in a low bush or tree. Three to 6 light green, speckled eggs are laid and the newly hatched young may appear as early as the third week in May.

Some redpolls move south in the fall to southern Canada and the northern United States.

The northern wheatear is about 15 cm in length with long wings, a short tail, and a thin bill. The underparts are buffy white, the back and head are white, and the face has a black mask around the eyes. In flight, the tail shows a distinctive black and white pattern. Like all thrushes, it has a melodious song of mixed harsh and pleasant notes.

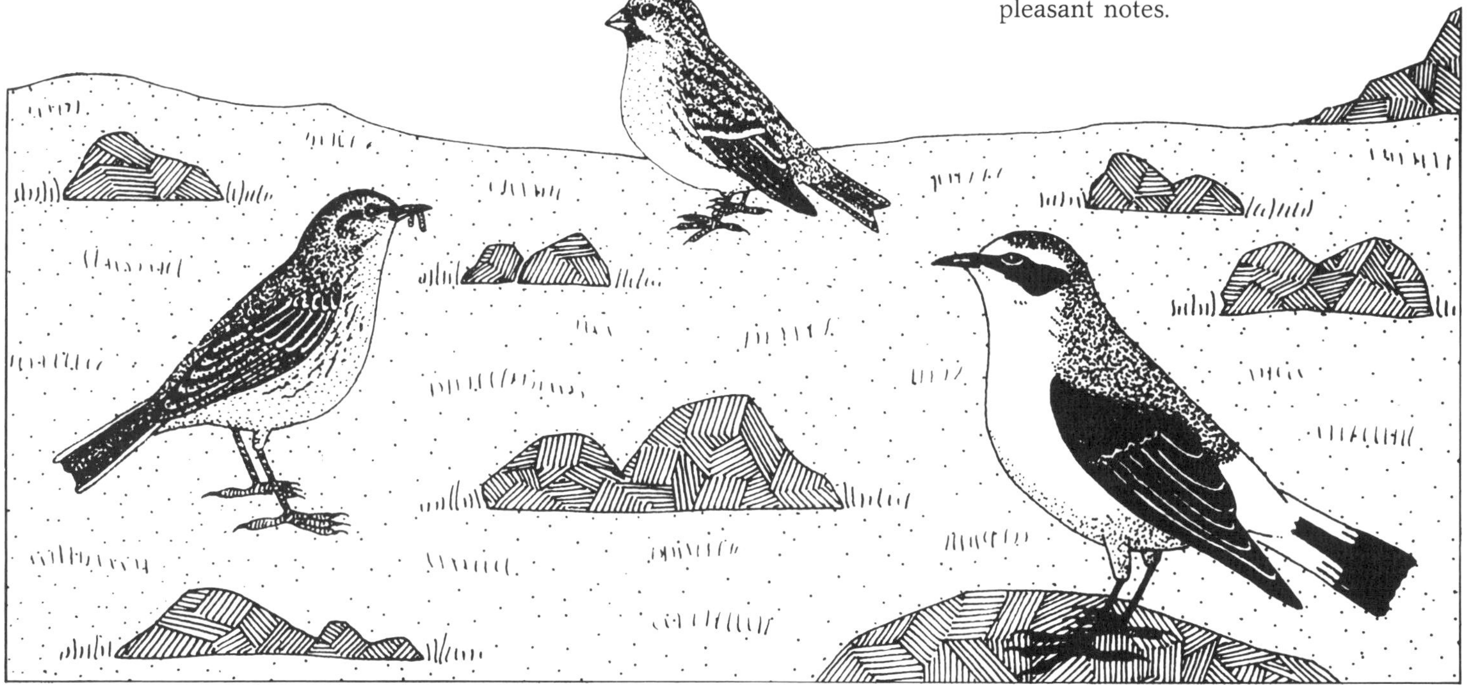

WATER PIPIT (left)	ᑯᔭᒥᖅᑕᖅ ᓯᐅᓯᐅᖅ	Kujamiqtaq Siusiuk	*Anthus spinoletta*
REDPOLL (centre)	ᓴᖅᑯᐊᕆᐊᖅ ᓯᖅᓯᒋᐊᖅ	Saqquariaq Siqsigiaq	*Carduelis* sp.
NORTHERN WHEATEAR (right)	ᐃᖁᓕᒐᖅ	Iquligaq	*Oenanthe oenanthe*

Northern wheatears breed on Southampton, Ellesmere and Baffin Islands, and possibly on the mainland around Rankin Inlet. They are ground-dwelling birds which prefer open terrain with rocks, ravines and shrubs. Nests are usually hidden under a rock, in a crevice, or in a hole in the ground. They are made of grass or moss and lined with feathers or hair. Five to 7 pale blue eggs are laid and incubation lasts for about two weeks.

Northern wheatears leave their breeding grounds in the eastern arctic in late August or early September and travel across the Atlantic to winter in Europe or Africa.

Lapland longspurs, redpolls, and snow buntings all belong to the finch family. One of the features they share is the shape of their beaks, which are stout and conical. The horned lark, which belongs to a different family, is often seen together with longspurs and buntings.

SNOW BUNTING   ⊲ᒪᐅᑕᑊ ᑨ⊲ᑦ   Amauligjuaq   *Plectrophenax nivalis*
                ᕴᐅ ᒡᕴᑦᖮᑦ   Qaulluqtaaq
                ᕴᑐ<ᑐ⊲ᑦ   Qupanuaq
                ⊲ᔅ ᓇ⋀⊲ᑦ   Arnaviaq

(male left, female right)

In southern Canada the arrival of the snow bunting is a sure sign of winter. In the north we look for them as a harbinger of spring. Generally appearing in flocks of hundreds or thousands near the treeline in mid-April, they continue on into the arctic where they breed from central Keewatin north to Ellesmere Island.

In breeding plumage the male is pure white with a black back, bill, and legs. The wings are mostly white with black tips but overhead the birds appear to be snow white. Females are similar, but have a distinct rusty tinge, especially on top of the head.

The birds are often seen in flocks and the song in flight is a short, slightly rising, musical twitter which frequently ends in a sharp "chert". On the breeding ground they warble a loud musical song.

Snow buntings nest in rock crevices and under stone and rock piles. The nest is made of moss and grasses, and is lined with grasses, feathers, and hair. Up to 7 greyish-white or bluish-white eggs are laid and the young hatch in just under 2 weeks.

Migration begins in mid-September and by early October most of the flocks are well south of the treeline. Snow buntings winter in all of southern Canada and as far north as the central part of the prairie provinces. In mild years some may overwinter in parts of the Northwest Territories.

Loons	red-throated loon	*Gavia stellata*
	arctic loon	*Gavia arctica*
	common loon	*Gavia immer*
	yellow-billed loon	*Gavia adamsii*
Tube-Nosed Swimmers	northern fulmar	*Fulmarus glacialis*
Waterfowl	tundra swan	*Cygnus columbianus*
	white-fronted goose	*Anser albifrons*
	snow goose	*Chen caerulescens*
	Ross's goose	*Chen rossii*
	brant	*Branta bernicla*
	Canada goose	*Branta canadensis*
	+green-winged teal	*Anas crecca*
	+mallard	*Anas platyrhynchos*
	pintail	*Anas acuta*
	+wigeon	*Anas americana*
	+greater scaup	*Aythya marila*
	common eider	*Somateria mollissima*
	king eider	*Somateria spectabilis*
	harlequin duck	*Histrionicus histrionicus*
	oldsquaw	*Clangula hyemalis*
	+white-winged scoter	*Melanitta fusca*
	red-breasted merganser	*Mergus serrator*
Diurnal Birds of Prey	rough-legged hawk	*Buteo lagopus*
	golden eagle	*Aquila chrysaetos*
	peregrine falcon	*Falco peregrinus*
	gyrfalcon	*Falco rusticolus*
Grouse & Ptarmigan	*willow ptarmigan	*Lagopus lagopus*
	*rock ptarmigan	*Lagopus mutus*
Cranes & Rails	sandhill crane	*Grus canadensis*
Gulls, Shorebirds, Alcids	black-bellied plover	*Pluvialis squatarola*
	American golden plover	*Pluvialis dominica*
	ringed plover	*Charadrius hiaticula*
	semipalmated plover	*Charadrius semipalmatus*
	+lesser yellowlegs	*Tringa flavipes*
	Eskimo curlew	*Numenius borealis*
	whimbrel	*Numenius phaeopus*
	Hudsonian godwit	*Limosa haemastica*
	ruddy turnstone	*Arenaria interpres*
	knot	*Calidris canutus*
	sanderling	*Calidris alba*
	semipalmated sandpiper	*Calidris pusilla*
	least sandpiper	*Calidris minutilla*
	white-rumped sandpiper	*Calidris fuscicollis*
	Baird's sandpiper	*Calidris bairdii*
	pectoral sandpiper	*Calidris melanotos*
	purple sandpiper	*Calidris maritima*

	dunlin	*Calidris alpina*
	stilt sandpiper	*Calidris himantopus*
	buff-breasted sandpiper	*Tryngites subrufricollis*
	+long-billed dowitcher	*Limnodromus scolopaceus*
	common snipe	*Gallinago gallinago*
	northern phalarope	*Phalaropus lobatus*
	red phalarope	*Phalaropus fulicaria*
	pomarine jaeger	*Stercorarius pomarinus*
	parasitic jaeger	*Stercorarius parasiticus*
	long-tailed jaeger	*Stercorarius longicaudus*
	herring gull	*Larus argentatus*
	Thayer's gull	*Larus thayeri*
	Iceland gull	*Larus glaucoides*
	glaucous gull	*Larus hyperboreus*
	black-legged kittiwake	*Rissa tridactyla*
	Ross's gull	*Rhodostethia rosea*
	Sabine's gull	*Xema sabini*
	ivory gull	*Pagophila eburnea*
	arctic tern	*Sterna paradisaea*
	dovekie	*Alle alle*
	thick-billed murre	*Uria lomvia*
	razorbill	*Alca torda*
	black guillemot	*Cepphus grylle*
Owls	*snowy owl	*Nyctea scandiaca*
	short-eared owl	*Asio flammeus*
Perching Birds	horned lark	*Eremophila alpestris*
	cliff swallow	*Hirundo pyrrhonota*
	*raven	*Corvus corax*
	wheatear	*Oenanthe oenanthe*
	gray-cheeked thrush	*Catharus minimus*
	robin	*Turdus migratorius*
	water pipit	*Anthus spinoletta*
	tree sparrow	*Spizella arborea*
	savannah sparrow	*Passerculus sandwichensis*
	+fox sparrow	*Passerella iliaca*
	white-crowned sparrow	*Zonotrichia leucophrys*
	Harris's sparrow	*Zonotrichia querula*
	Lapland longspur	*Calcarius lapponicus*
	Smith's longspur	*Calcarius pictus*
	snow bunting	*Plectrophenax nivalis*
	common redpoll	*Carduelis flammea*
	hoary redpoll	*Carduelis hornemanni*

* species which overwinter

+ species whose occurrence above the treeline is mainly in the area of Tuktoyaktuk Peninsula and/or Anderson River

FISH

Fish were the first vertebrates to evolve, and from them all other forms of vertebrate life developed. Unlike mammals and birds, which they still outnumber, they have no lungs, taking oxygen from the water directly into the bloodstream by means of gills. Most fishes have an air bladder which is used to regulate buoyancy. Scales (which in many species can be used to determine age by counting growth rings) are often but not always present.

Fish have an extremely well-developed sense of smell. They also have senses of taste, sight and hearing. Their sense of touch is generally poor, except in those fish possessing barbels, which help locate food by touch. They also have "skin senses," such as the lateral line system seen in many fishes. This is a line of pores along each side of the body used for detecting changes in pressure and temperature.

The distribution of fishes is restricted by a variety of conditions, including temperature, light and salinity. Some species are benthic (bottom-dwelling) in nature, while others are pelagic (swimming about freely). Most fishes inhabit either freshwater or salt water, but some spend part of their life cycle in both. Fish which live in salt water and migrate up rivers to spawn are termed "anadromous".

Much information has been gathered on freshwater fishes occurring in the Northwest Territories, but marine fishes are less well-known. This is because freshwater species are generally more accessible, and therefore of greater importance nutritionally and economically in the arctic.

Kingdom
Animalia
(all animals)

Kingdom
Plantae
(all plants)

Phylum
Chordata
(animals with notochords)

Phylum
Mollusca
(clams, snails, octopus, etc.)

Phylum
Arthropoda
(insects, spiders crustaceans)

Phylum
Annelida
(segmented worms)

Phylum
Nematoda
(roundworms)

Phylum
Platyhelminthes
(flatworms)

Phylum
Cnideria
(corals & jellyfish)

Phylum
Porifera
(sponges)

Phylum
Protozoa
(single-celled animals)

Class
Osteichthyes
(bony fishes)

Class
Chondrichthyes
(cartilaginous fishes: sharks & rays)

Class
Agnatha
(jawless fishes: hagfishes & lampreys)

Class
Reptilia
(reptiles)

Class
Amphibia
(amphibians)

Class
Aves
(birds)

Class
Mammalia
(mammals)

Order
Clupeiformes
(herrings)

Order
Cypriniformes
(including chubs & suckers)

Order
Gasterosteiformes
(sticklebacks)

Order
Myctophiformes
(including lanternfish)

Order
Gadiformes
(cods & others)

Order
Perciformes
(spiny-rayed fishes)

Order
Pleuronectiformes
(flatfishes)

Order
Salmoniformes
(trout-like fishes)

Family
Gadidae
(cods)

Family
Agonidae
(poachers & alligatorfish)

Family
Cyclopteridae
(snailfishes)

Family
Salmonidae
(ciscoes, whitefishes, salmons, trouts, char, grayling)

Family
Macrouridae
(grenadiers)

Family
Ammodytidae
(sand lances)

Family
Pholidae
(gunnels)

Family
Osmeridae
(smelts, capelin)

Family
Zoarcidae
(eelpouts)

Family
Anarhichadidae
(wolffishes)

Family
Scorpaenidae
(including redfish)

Family
Esocidae
(pikes)

Family
Cottidae
(sculpins)

Family
Stichaeidae
(pricklebacks)

Simplified diagram showing most orders and families of fishes found in freshwater above the treeline, and in marine waters of the Northwest Territories, and their relationship to other organisms.

ARCTIC CHAR

Arctic char are the most northerly of all freshwater fish. They are found in coastal areas throughout the arctic archipelago, and in many lakes and rivers on arctic islands and the mainland. Except in the larger rivers, however, they seldom range far inland.

The arctic char comes in a broad range of colours. It may be a uniform silver, or it may have an olive-green or deep blue back, white belly and pinkish spots along the sides. At breeding time the sides, underparts and lower fins of males turn a bright orange-red.

Some live permanently in freshwater lakes, while others are anadromous, which means they swim downstream to the sea in spring and return upriver in autumn to spawn. They may reach over 90 cm in length and weigh up to 11 or 12 kg, but generally are much smaller. Sea-run fish commonly weigh 2-5 kg, while landlocked char are less. The largest char on record was caught at Tree River and weighed just under 15 kg.

Their diet is quite varied, with principal food items varying from area to area depending on availability. It includes insects, plankton, algae, small fish and invertebrates called amphipods and mysids.

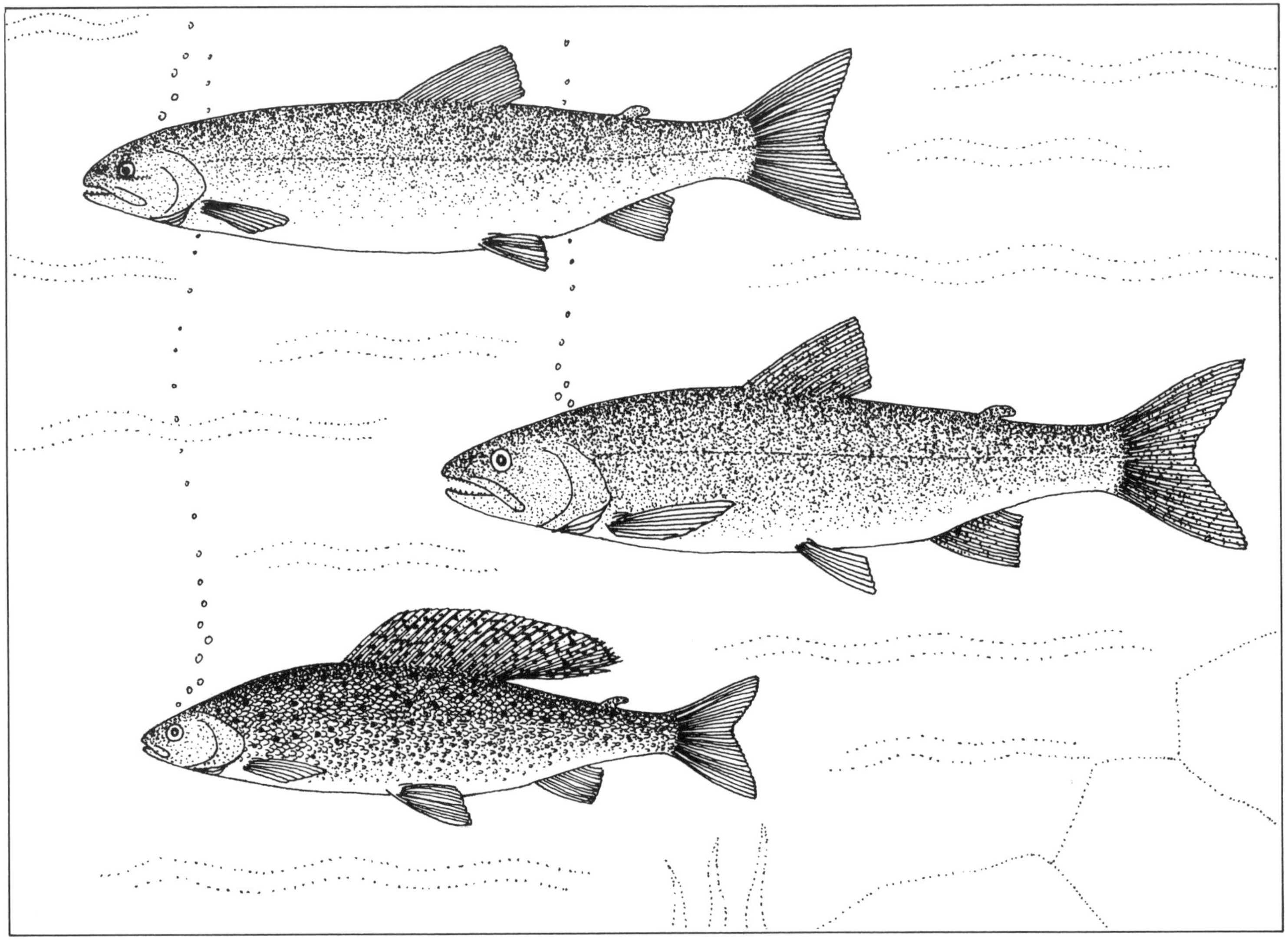

ARCTIC CHAR (top)	ᐃᖃᓗᒃ	Iqaluk	*Salvelinus alpinus*
Arctic char in sea	ᑕᕆᐅᕐᒥᐅᑕᖅ	Tariurmiutaq	
Non-spawning adult (silver)	ᑲᕙᓯᓕᒃ /ᑲᕕᓯᓕᒃ	Kavasilik / *Kavisilik*	
Spawning adult (red)	ᐃᕕᑖᕈᖅ /ᐃᕕᓵᕈᖅ ᑕᕆᐅᕐᒧᐊᕈᓐᓇ-ᓐᖏᑦᑐᖅ	Ivitaaruq / Ivisaaruq Tariurmuarunnanngit-tuq	
Landlocked char	ᓄᑎᓕᐊᕐᔪᒃ / ᑎᓱᔪᐃᑦᑐᖅ	Nutiliarjuk / Tisujuittuq	
Spring-run char	ᓯᑐᐊᔪᖅ /ᑭᓱᐊᔪᖅ ᓯᑐᓕᖅᑐᖅ /ᑎᓱᐊᔪᖅ	Situajuq / Kisuajuq Situliqtuq / Tisuajuq	
Fall-run char	ᒪᔪᖅᑐᖅ /ᒪᔪᓕᖅᑐᖅ	Majuqtuq / Majuliqtuq	
Fingerling	ᐃᖃᓗᒐᖅ	Iqalugaq	
LAKE TROUT (centre)	ᐃᓘᕋᖅ ᐃᓲᕋᖅ	Iłuuraq Isuuraq	*Salvelinus namaycush*
ARCTIC GRAYLING (bottom)	ᓱᓗᒃᐸᐅᒐᖅ	Sulukpaugaq	*Thymallus arcticus*

Char reach sexual maturity at 7 years in the Keewatin and around 11 years in Baffin and the central arctic. They spawn in September or October at depths of 1-4.5 m every 2-4 years. The female clears a nest or redd in a gravel or rocky bottom with the action of her tail. She then lays several thousand eggs, which are fertilized by the male. The eggs are covered up and develop slowly during the winter until they hatch in the spring.

Char are fished commercially in several areas in the Northwest Territories. The greatest harvest comes from the Cambridge Bay area, where approximately 55,000 kg per year are taken. This is primarily for shipment to southern markets. On Baffin Island about 45,000 kg are harvested commercially every year, but this is used for intersettlement trade. A smaller commercial fishery takes place along the west coast of Hudson Bay in the area of Rankin Inlet.

Some well-known sport fishing areas include Victoria Island, Tree River (Coronation Gulf), Kolucktoo Bay (north Baffin), and Clearwater Fiord (south Baffin). Angling limits are 4 daily with a maximum possession of 7, except for certain designated waters.

Lake trout occur throughout the entire mainland and on Banks, Victoria and a few other islands. They inhabit large lakes and, unlike lake trout in southern Canada, are also found in shallow lakes and rivers. They are sometimes found in brackish coastal water, but are primarily a freshwater fish.

Their colour may be silver, green or dark purple. An orange colouration may suffuse the lower fins and tail. Like char, the flesh may be white or orange.

The largest lake trout on record weighed 46 kg and was taken by a gillnet in Lake Athabasca. The world's angling record is 29.5 kg and comes from Great Bear Lake.

Lake trout spawn in autumn in shallow water over rocky bottoms. They do not spawn until they are 6 or 7 years old (in Great Bear Lake, not until around 13 years of age). They do not spawn annually, but only every second or third year. The eggs remain on the bottom trapped in rocky crevices until late winter or spring.

Trout feed on a variety of organisms including insects, crustaceans, fish and even small mammals. Ciscoes are the preferred fish species eaten, but whitefish, sculpins, sticklebacks and others are also taken.

Lake trout used to be important commercially in Great Slave Lake but now are only incidentally taken there. Due to their slow growth rates and delayed maturity they do not respond well to commercial fishing. A lake trout in southern Canada may weigh two or three times as much as a trout of the same age in the Northwest Territories.

Their greatest value in the north lies in sport fishing. Angling limits are 3 daily with a maximum possession of 5, except for certain designated waters.

Arctic grayling are found throughout most of the mainland in the Northwest Territories, both above and below the treeline. They are not found on any of the arctic islands. They generally inhabit only those lakes and rivers with clear cold water. In large lakes they stay close to rocky shores and near the mouths of streams.

Their most distinctive feature is a large dorsal fin which in water ripples like an unfurled sail. The back is dark purple or bluish-black, shading to silver on the sides (speckled with a few black spots) and white below.

Grayling spawn in the spring during breakup. They migrate to small gravelly streams where they lay their eggs on the bottom without preparing a nest or redd. The average number of eggs laid is 4,000-7,000. They hatch in 2-3 weeks. Sexual maturity is usually reached at 6-9 years of age, while maximum age is about 11 or 12 years. The largest grayling on record weighed 2.7 kg and was 76 cm long. It was caught in a small river on the north shore of Great Bear Lake. Most grayling however are in the 1 kg and 30-40 cm range.

Grayling feed extensively on insects and as a result are one of the few species in the north which provide fly fishing. When hooked they are energetic fighters, putting up a good battle for their size. Their tendency to leap out of the water when caught, their readiness to take the hook, their soft mouth, their beauty and good taste, all make the grayling a popular sport fish. Catch limits everywhere above the treeline are 5 daily and total possession 10.

WHITEFISHES

Three types of whitefish are common in the Northwest Territories. Broad whitefish are found in drainages along the northwest coast of the mainland from the Mackenzie Delta to Bathurst Inlet. Lake whitefish and round whitefish are found throughout the entire mainland except in the northeastern Keewatin.

All are similar in appearance, being silvery-grey overall with a dark back. Broad whitefish are the largest. They are thick and heavy-set with a blunt snout and grow to a length of about 46 cm. Round whitefish are the smallest and more slender in shape than the others. They reach an average length of 20-30 cm. Lake whitefish grow to a length of about 38 cm, with adults often becoming hump-backed.

Whitefish are closely related to ciscoes, which belong to the same sub-family and are similar in appearance but much smaller. In addition, the position of the mouth is different. In whitefish it is placed below the point of the snout, while in ciscoes it is placed at the end of the snout. The reason for this difference is that

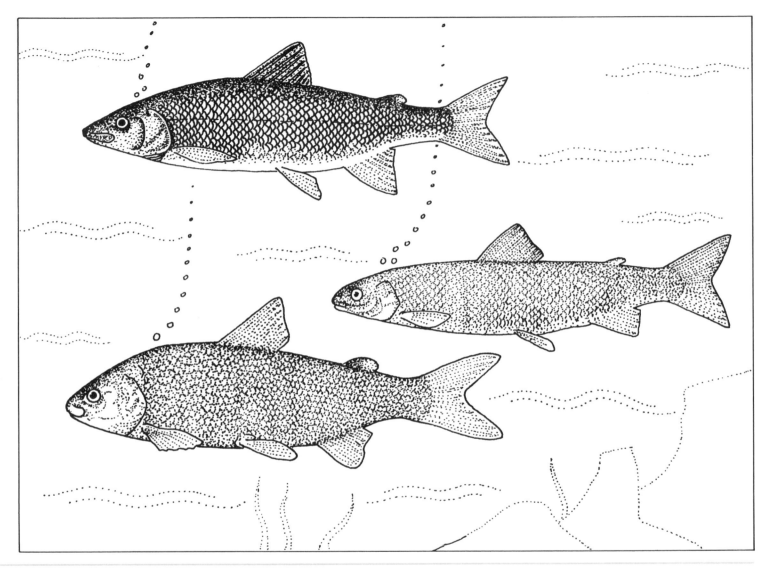

LAKE WHITEFISH (top)	ᑲᐱᓯᓕᒃ ᑲᕙᓯᓕᒃ	Kavisilik Kavasilik	*Coregonus clupeaformis*
ROUND WHITEFISH (centre)	ᑲᕙᓯᓕᒃ ᑲᐱᓯᓕᒃ	Kavasilik Kavisilik	*Prosopium cylindraceum*
BROAD WHITEFISH (bottom)	ᑲᐱᓯᓕᒃ ᑲᕙᓯᓕᒃ	Kavisilik Kavasilik	*Coregonus nasus*

whitefish are generally bottom feeders while ciscoes prey on organisms found in open water.

Whitefish are found in both lakes and rivers, sometimes in brakish waters of major drainages and occasionally in the sea. Broad whitefish are found most often in rivers, lake whitefish are found in most large lakes and large rivers, and round whitefish prefer shallow areas of lakes and clear streams.

All three species spawn in late summer or fall, shedding their eggs over gravel beds or rocks. Hatching occurs during April and May.

Lake whitefish are the most valuable commercial fish in the Northwest Territories, with the most important harvest location being Great Slave Lake. Whitefish adapt well to commercial fishing — their age of maturity decreases, their growth rate increases, and they produce more eggs.

Broad whitefish have only local commercial value, though many are taken in gill nets for domestic use. Round whitefish are of minor commercial value because of their small size and fluctuating supply.

Sticklebacks are small scaleless fishes characterized by the presence of a number of dorsal spines. The sides may be protected by bony plates. Of the two species found in the north, both are equally at home in fresh or salt water — though marine populations spawn in fresh water. They construct nests of vegetation using a kidney secretion to bind the material together. Despite their armor and pugnacious nature, they are important prey for many fishes, including trout, and for fish-eating birds.

The threespine stickleback is found in Hudson Bay, Hudson Strait and southern Baffin Island. It is armed with three dorsal spines and bears up to 30 bony plates on each side in marine populations, with fewer or none in freshwater populations. It does not usually exceed 76 mm in length.

Spawning occures in June or July. The male builds a nest shaped like a barrel, open at both ends. He remains with the nest after the eggs have been laid and fertilized, and guards the young after they hatch, which is in about 7 days.

The ninespine stickleback is found throughout the mainland as well as on Victoria and Baffin Islands. It bears nine dorsal spines as well as a number of small bony plates at the base of the dorsal fin, and in several places on the ventral surface. Length is about 64 mm.

Spawning occurs in the summer. As in the threespine stickleback, the male constructs the nest, and guards the eggs and young.

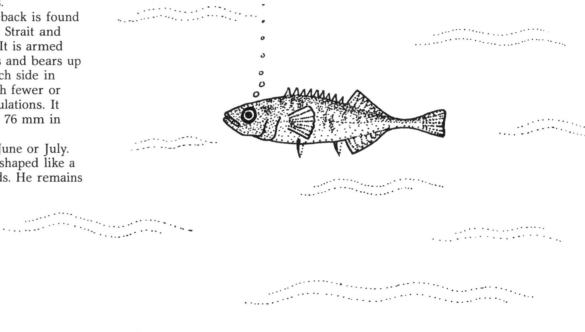

NINESPINE STICKLEBACK ᐸᑭᓴᒃ Kakilasak *Pungitius pungitius*
ᐸᑭᓴᒃ Kakilisak

SCULPINS

Sculpins are spiny fish with a large head tapering to a narrow tail. Both marine and freshwater species occur in the Northwest Territories. Freshwater varieties are 5-10 cm in length, while marine varieties are generally larger at 10-50 cm. Most sculpins are bottom feeders, living on aquatic insects, larvae, plankton and crustaceans. Sculpins have no value as food for humans, but they are important in the diet of many other fish.

Three species are found in freshwater above the treeline: the slimy sculpin, the spoonhead sculpin, and the deepwater sculpin. The first occurs throughout the mainland except in the northeastern Keewatin, while the second is found in central Keewatin. The third occurs in Great Slave and Great Bear Lakes, as well as on Victoria Island.

At least nine species of sculpins are found in arctic marine waters: rough hookear, arctic staghorn, twohorn, fourhorn, shorthorn, spatulate, arctic, mailed and ribbed.

SHARKS

Sharks belong to a group of fishes known as cartilaginous fish. They have cartilage rather than bones in their skeletons and are considered more primitive than bony fishes. Males are equipped with claspers — curled tubelike extensions of their pelvic fins — which transport sperm to effect internal fertilization. They may be born alive or hatched from eggs externally, depending on the species.

Two species are found in arctic waters: the black dogfish and the Greenland shark. The former is found only in Davis Strait, while the latter occurs in Baffin Bay, Davis Strait and Hudson Strait.

The black dogfish is a small shark, averaging only 60-75 cm in length. Both its dorsal fins are preceded by a stout spine. In Canadian waters it is usually caught at depths of 450 m or greater.

The Greenland shark grows to lengths of 7 m and weights of 1 tonne. It is almost entirely an arctic species, being found only rarely in temperate waters and then only at depths of over 500 m. In the arctic it often swims near the surface, where it feeds on a wide variety of fish as well as seals and seabirds. It has been fished commercially for many years with as many as 50,000 taken annually in the early part of the century off Greenland. The oil from its liver was used for fuel and as much as 140 litres of it could be obtained from a large shark. The flesh is edible but must be dried first to eliminate the effects of urea, which is found in the blood in very high levels.

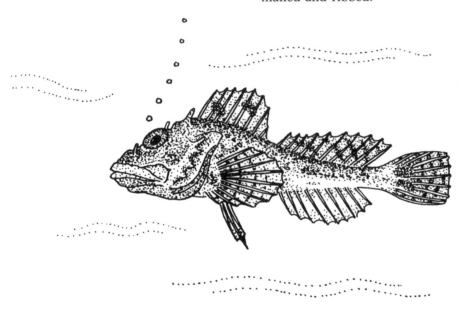

SCULPINS   ᐸᐅᔪᖅ   Kanajuq   Family *Cottidae*

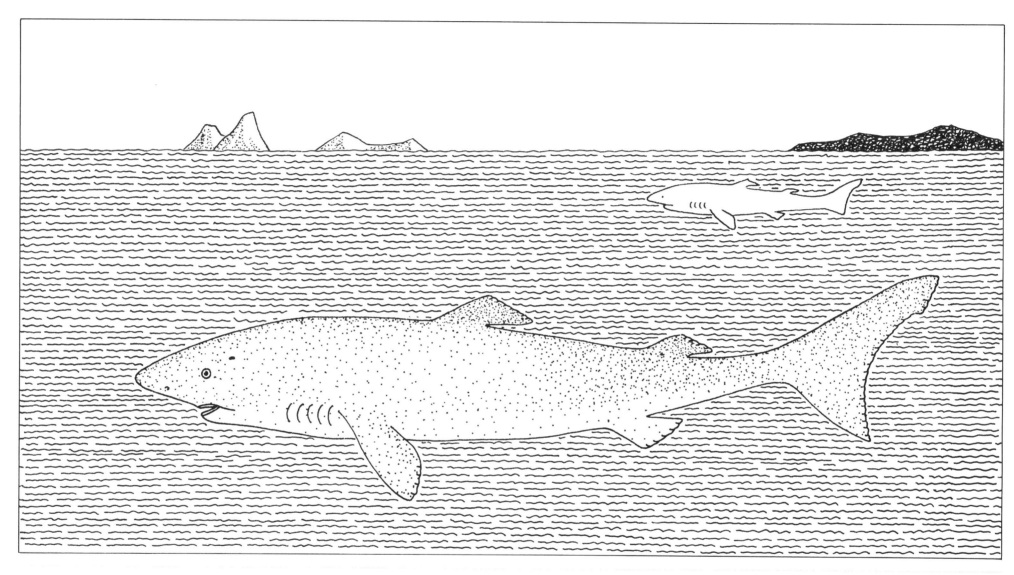

GREENLAND SHARK   ᐃᖃᓗᒍᔪᐊᖅ   Iqalugjuaq   *Somniosus microcephalus*

Flatfishes are edible marine fishes, with many species sharing a few well-known common names (such as sole, flounder, and halibut). They are also one of the oddest groups of fishes inhabiting our seas. Although they begin life swimming about in a normal manner, they soon undergo a drastic change in appearance and behaviour. They lie and swim on one side, with the lower side losing its pigment and the lower eye migrating to the upper side. The eyes can be elevated slightly and moved independently, resulting in a somewhat crazed appearance. Flatfishes rest on either the right or left side, depending on the species. They are found on sandy or muddy bottoms, where they feed mainly on invertebrates.

Three species are found in various arctic waters: arctic flounder, starry flounder, and Greenland halibut. All are alike in general appearance, being flat and oval-shaped, with long continuous dorsal and anal fins, and their eyes on the right side.

The Greenland halibut is found in the north Atlantic off the coast of Greenland and Baffin Island. It is a deepwater fish, growing to lengths of 1 m and weights of over 10 kg. It is distinguished from all other flatfishes (except the Atlantic halibut) by its tail, which is slightly concave rather than rounded. Farther south it is fished commercially, but marketed under the name "Greenland turbot".

Lumpfishes are carnivorous marine fishes found in the northern hemisphere. Their pelvic fins are modified to form a round sucking disc under their body which is used to attach themselves to rocks on the bottom. The body is rounded rather than elongated, and covered with warty tubercles and cone-shaped projections. Although most members of this family are rather small, lumpfishes as long as 60 cm and weighing 6 kg have been recorded.

Three species occur in arctic waters: the lumpfish, found in Hudson Bay; the leatherfin lumpsucker, found in Hudson Bay and Hudson Strait; and the Atlantic spiny lumpsucker, found in a variety of locations throughout the arctic, including Prince Patrick Island, Jones Sound, Lake Harbour, and Hudson Bay.

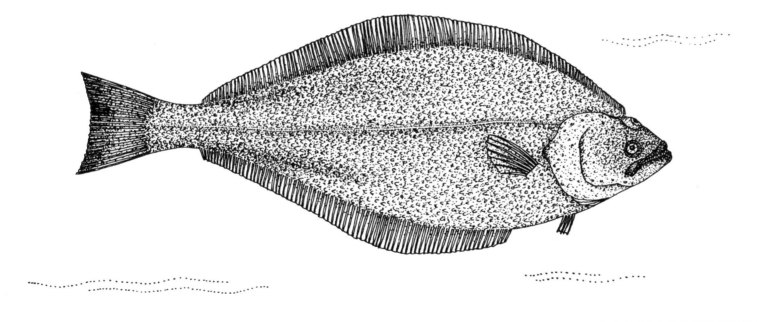

GREENLAND HALIBUT ᐊᑕᖅᓇᖅ Natarnaq *Reinhardtius*
ᑎᒃᑲᓕᒃ Tikkalik *hippoglossoides*

Lumpfish are frequently preyed upon by seals. They inhabit rocky waters to depths of about 150 m, often where currents are fast-moving. The eggs are laid in shallow water and guarded by the male. In Europe, where they are called henfish, several million kilograms are consumed annually.

Cods are primarily marine fishes. In their most typical forms they possess three dorsal fins and two anal fins, or long continuous dorsal and anal fins of even height, resulting in a somewhat sinuous appearance. The head is typically large and a single barbel is suspended from the chin. They feed heavily on other fishes and on invertebrates. The eggs of marine varieties contain an oil globule which causes them to float near the ocean's surface. There are six species present in arctic marine waters: polar, arctic, saffron, Atlantic, ogac or Greenland cod, and threebeard rockling.

The arctic cod occurs almost exclusively in the Arctic Ocean. It prefers very cold water and is often found among ice floes near shore, or in the layer of water just below the sea ice — though it may also be found in depths up to 700 m.

LUMPFISH (left)　σΛ˥　Nipisa　*Cyclopterus lumpus*

ARCTIC COD (right)　ᐲᒡᖅ　Uugaq　*Boreogadus saida*

Spawning occurs in January and February with the young emerging in April or May, and later in heavy ice areas. During the first few months they grow rapidly and are 60-75 mm long by the end of the first year. However, growth slows after the second year and few arctic cod grow beyond 30 cm or live beyond 7 years of age.

Burbot are freshwater cod, though they are sometimes found in brackish coastal waters. They are found throughout the mainland except in the northeastern Keewatin. In some parts of the world they can weigh up to 34 kg and measure up to 122 cm in length. In Canada, the maximum size is about 95 cm. The record from Great Slave Lake is 8.4 kg and 94 cm.

Burbot are present in the deep waters of lakes and large cool rivers where they prey on insects, deepwater invertebrates and other fish. They spawn in lake shallows under the ice in mid to late winter. Breeding occurs at night in groups of several males and females, which writhe together in a ball over the bottom. The eggs, as many as a million from a single female, are shed over the bottom and the young hatch in about a month.

Burbot are generally considered to be a coarse fish. They are said to have a rather insipid flavour in summer, but the roe can be made into biscuits, and oil from the liver, which has a rich delicate flavour and is high in vitamins A and D, can be taken like cod-liver oil. In winter, the flesh of the burbot is white, firm and of a better flavour.

BURBOT   ∩ᐧĊᑕᐧ   Tiktaalik   *Lota lota*

		Freshwater only	Primarily freshwater but occasionally found in coastal waters	Anadromous, but also with freshwater populations
Arctic char	*Salvelinus alpinus*			•
Lake trout	*Salvelinus namaycush*		•	
Cisco	*Coregonus artedii*		•	
Arctic cisco	*Coregonus autumnalis*			•
Least cisco	*Coregonus sardinella*			•
Lake whitefish	*Coregonus clupeaformis*		•	
Broad whitefish	*Corregonus nasus*		•	
Round whitefish	*Prosopium cylindraceum*	•		
Inconnu	*Stenodus leucichthys*			•
Arctic grayling	*Thymallus arcticus*	•		
Rainbow smelt	*Osmerus mordax*			•
Northern pike	*Esox lucius*	•		
Lake chub	*Couesius plumbeus*	•		
Longnose sucker	*Catostomus catostomus*		•	
Burbot	*Lota lota*	•		
Threespine stickleback	*Gasterosteus aculeatus*			•
Ninespine stickleback	*Pungitius pungitius*			•
Slimy sculpin	*Cottus cognatus*	•		
Spoonhead sculpin	*Cottus ricei*		•	
Deepwater sculpin	*Myoxocephalus thompsoni*	•		

Cods
- polar cod — *Arctogadus glacialis*
- arctic cod — *Boreogadus saida*
- saffron cod — *Eleginus gracilis*
- Atlantic cod — *Gadus morhua*
- Greenland cod — *Gadus ogac*
- threebeard rockling — *Gaidropsarus ensis*

Pricklebacks
- blackline prickleback — *Acantholumpenus mackayi*
- Yarrell's blenny — *Chirolophus ascani*
- fourline snakeblenny — *Eumesogrammus praecisus*
- slender eelblenny — *Lumpenus fabricii*
- daubed shanny — *Lumpenus maculatus*
- snakeblenny — *Lumpenus lumpretaeformis*

Eelpouts
- fish doctor — *Gymnelis viridis*
- shulupaoluk — *Lycodes jugoricus*
- pale eelpout — *Lycodes pallidus*
- arctic eelpout — *Lycodes reticulatus*
- polar eelpout — *Lycodes turneri*

Sculpins
- rough hookear — *Artediellus scaber*
- arctic staghorn sculpin — *Gymnocanthus tricuspis*
- twohorn sculpin — *Icelus bicornis*
- spatulate sculpin — *Icelus spatula*
- fourhorn sculpin — *Myoxocephalus quadricornis*
- arctic sculpin — *Myoxocephalus scorpioides*
- shorthorn sculpin — *Myoxocephalus scorpius*
- mailed sculpin — *Triglops murrayi*
- ribbed sculpin — *Triglops pingeli*

Lumpfishes & Snailfishes
- lumpfish — *Cyclopterus lumpus*
- leatherfin lumpsucker — *Eumicrotremus derjugini*
- Atlantic spiny lumpsucker — *Eumicrotremus spinosus*
- polka-dot snailfish — *Liparis cyclostigma*
- gelatinous seasnail — *Liparis koefoedi*
- striped seasnail — *Liparis liparis*
- bartail snailfish — *Liparis herschelinus*

Flatfishes
- arctic flounder — *Liopsetta glacialis*
- starry flounder — *Platichthys stellatus*
- Greenland halibut — *Reinhardtius hippoglossoides*

Other Fishes
- Atlantic sea poacher — *Agonus decagonus*
- arctic alligatorfish — *Aspidophoroides olriki*
- northern sand lance — *Ammodytes dubius*
- Pacific sand lance — *Ammodytes hexapterus*
- northern wolffish — *Anarhichas denticulatus*
- glacier lanternfish — *Benthosema glaciale*
- black dogfish — *Centroscyllium fabricii*
- Greenland shark — *Somniosus microcephalus*
- Atlantic herring — *Clupea harengus harengus*
- Pacific herring — *Clupea harengus pallasi*
- rock grenadier (or rat-tail) — *Coryphaenoides rupestris*
- capelin — *Mallotus villosus*
- northern hagfish — *Myxine glutinosa*
- banded gunnel — *Pholis fasciata*
- redfish — *Sebastes mentella*

Selected Bibliography

Terrestrial Mammals

Banfield, A.W.F. 1974. *The Mammals of Canada.* University of Toronto Press, Toronto.

Burt, William H. and Richard P. Grossenheider. 1976. *A Field Guide to the Mammals.* Houghton Mifflin Co., Boston.

Calef, George. 1981. *Caribou and the Barren-Lands.* CARC/Firefly Books, Ottawa/Toronto.

Carbyn, L.N. (ed.). 1983. *Wolves in Canada and Alaska: Their Status, Biology and Management.* Canadian Wildlife Service, Ottawa.

Chapman, Joseph A. and George A. Feldhamer (eds.). 1982. *Wild Mammals of North America.* Johns Hopkins University Press, Baltimore.

Dickinson, D.M. and T.B. Herman. 1979. *Management of Some Terrestrial Mammals in the Northwest Territories.* Science Advisory Board of the Northwest Territories, Yellowknife.

Harper, Francis. 1956. *The Mammals of Keewatin.* University of Kansas; Lawrence, Ks.

Rue, Leonard Lee III. 1981. *Furbearing Animals of North America.* Crown Publishers Inc., New York.

Savage, Arthur and Candace Savage. 1981. *Wild Mammals of Western Canada.* Western Producer Prairie Books, Saskatoon.

Schmidt, John L. and Douglas L. Gilbert. 1978. *Big Game of North America.* Stackpole Books; Harrisburg, Pa.

Tinling, R. 1982. *Northwest Territories Fur Production 1957-58 to 1978-79.* Northwest Territories Department of Renewable Resources, Yellowknife.

Urquhart, D.R. 1982. *Muskox: Life History and Current Status of Muskoxen in the N.W.T.* Northwest Territories Dept. of Renewable Resources, Yellowknife.

Urquhart, D.R. and R.E. Schweinsburg. 1984. *Polar Bear: Life History and Known Distribution of Polar Bear in the Northwest Territorites up to 1981.* Northwest Territories Dept. of Renewable Resources, Yellowknife.

Whitaker, John O. Jr. (ed.). 1980. *The Audubon Society Field Guide to North American Mammals.* Alfred A. Knopf, New York.

Wooding, Frederick H. 1982. *Wild Mammals of Canada.* McGraw-Hill Ryerson, Toronto.

Marine Mammals

Banfield, A.W.F. 1974. *The Mammals of Canada.* University of Toronto Press, Toronto.

Burton, Robert. 1980. *The Life and Death of Whales.* Andre Deutsch Ltd., London.

Chapman, Joseph A. and George A. Feldhamer (eds.). 1982. *Wild Mammals of North America.* John Hopkins University Press, Baltimore.

Coffey, D.J. 1977. *Dolphins, Whales and Porpoises: An Encyclopedia of Sea Mammals.* Collier Books, New York.

Davis, Rolph A., Kerwin J. Finley and W. John Richardson. 1980. *The Present Status and Future Management of Arctic Marine Mammals in Canada.* Science Advisory Board of the Northwest Territories, Yellowknife.

Mansfield, A.W. 1967. *Seals of Arctic and Eastern Canada.* Fisheries Research Board of Canada, Ottawa.

Matthews, L. Harrison. 1978. *The Natural History of the Whale.* Weidenfeld and Nicolson, London.

Birds

American Ornithologists' Union. 1983. *Check-list of North American Birds.* (6th edition). Allen Press; Lawrence, Ks.

Bellrose, Frank C. 1976. *Ducks, Geese and Swans of North America.* Stackpole Books; Harrisburg, Pa.

Bull, John and John Farrand, Jr. 1977. *The Audubon Society Field Guide to North American Birds: Eastern Region.* Alfred A. Knopf, New York.

Godfrey, W. Earl. 1966. *The Birds of Canada.* National Museums of Canada, Ottawa.

Harrison, Colin. 1978. *A Field Guide to the Nests, Eggs and Nestlings of North American Birds.* Collins, Glasgow.

Heintzelman, Donald S. 1979. *Hawks and Owls of North America.* Universe Books, New York.

Manning, T. H. *Birds of the West James Bay and Southern Hudson Bay Coasts.* National Museum of Canada, Ottawa.

Mansell, William and Gary Low. 1980. *North American Birds of Prey.* Gage Publishing Ltd., Toronto.

Ogilvie, M.A. 1978. *Wild Geese.* Buteo Books; Vermillion, South Dakota.

Peterson, Roger Tory. 1980. *A Field Guide to the Birds.* (4th edition). Houghton Mifflin Co., Boston.

Salt, W. Ray and Jim R. Salt. 1976. *The Birds of Alberta.* Hurtig Publishers, Edmonton.

Terres, John K. 1980. *The Audubon Society Encyclopedia of North American Birds.* Alfred A. Knopf, New York.

Fish

Corkum, L.D. and P.J. McCart. 1981. *A Review of the Fisheries of the Mackenzie Delta and Nearshore Beaufort Sea.* Canadian Manuscript Report of Fisheries and Aquatic Sciences No. 1613.

Leim, A.H. and W.R. Scott. 1966. *Fishes of the Atlantic Coast of Canada.* Fisheries Research Board of Canada, Ottawa.

McCart, P.J. and J. Den Beste. 1979. *Aquatic Resources of the Northwest Territories.* Science Advisory Board of the Northwest Territories, Yellowknife.

McPhail, J.D. and C.C. Lindsey. 1970. *Freshwater Fishes of Northwestern Canada and Alaska.* Fisheries Research Board of Canada, Ottawa.

Robbins, C. Richard, Reeve M. Bailey, Carl E. Bond, James R. Brooker, Ernest A. Lachner, Robert N. Lea and W.R. Scott. 1980. *A List of Common and Scientific Names of Fishes from the United States and Canada.* (4th edition). American Fisheries Society, Bethesda, Md.

Scott, W.B. and E.J. Crossman. 1973. *Freshwater Fishes of Canada.* Fisheries Research Board of Canada, Ottawa.

Others

Anonymous. 1982. *Environmental Impact Statement for Hydrocarbon Development in the Beaufort Sea — Mackenzie Delta Region. Volume 3B: Northwest Passage Setting.* Dome Petroleum Ltd., Esso Resources Canada Ltd., and Gulf Canada Resources Inc.

Ray, G. Carleton and M.G. McCormick-Ray. 1981. *Wildlife of the Polar Regions.* Harry N. Abrams Inc., New York.

Wilkinson, Douglas. 1970. *The Arctic Coast.* N.S.L. Natural Science of Canada Ltd., Toronto.

Zoltai, S.C., K.J. McCormick and G.W. Scotter. 1983. *A Natural Resource Survey of Bylot Island and Adjacent Baffin Island, Northwest Territories.* Parks Canada.